GROWING CITIZENS

GROWING CITIZENS

Editors

ALISON ELLIOT and HEIDI POON

CENTRE FOR THEOLOGY AND PUBLIC ISSUES
NEW COLLEGE
THE UNIVERSITY OF EDINBURGH

SAINT ANDREW PRESS
Edinburgh

First published in 2009 by
SAINT ANDREW PRESS
121 George Street
Edinburgh EH2 4YN

ISBN 978 0 7152 0872 4

British Library Cataloguing in Publication Data
A catalogue record for this book is available from the British Library

It is the publisher's policy to only use papers that are natural and recyclable and that have been manufactured from timber grown in renewable, properly managed forests. All of the manufacturing processes of the papers are expected to conform to the environmental regulations of the country of origin.

Typeset in Sabon by Waverley Typesetters, Fakenham
Manufactured in Great Britain by Bell & Bain Ltd, Glasgow

Contents

Introduction

What is citizenship and how can we nurture good citizens?

The story of this book started as a consultation in June 2002, on the discussion paper by Learning and Teaching Scotland that was proposing a new framework for citizenship education for Scottish schools. It was hosted by the Centre for Theology and Public Issues (CTPI) of the University of Edinburgh, a centre which explores, through conferences and research, areas of public policy to which theology can make a distinctive contribution. At that period, the Centre was taking citizenship as its theme, inspired by the closeness of the newly restored Scottish Parliament, which was meeting at that time in the same complex of buildings as CTPI. Churches had been active in the campaign for the Parliament, contributing theological understandings of the nature of sovereignty to the drive for this constitutional change. CTPI initiated various research strands, including a study of the role of new media in contemporary citizenship, which culminated in the publication *Netting Citizens*,[1] a companion volume to this one.

A more extensive conference on citizenship education was held in November 2003, supported by the Christendom Trust (now MB Reckitt Trust), with the title 'Growing

Citizens'. A feature of this conference was a programme of imaginative workshops, introducing participants to the possibility of teaching philosophy to children in primary schools, exploring the attitudes schools adopted to their students taking part in protest marches, and learning about community education projects on environmental justice. The present volume of reflective essays on aspects of citizenship education arose out of this event, with most of the chapters commissioned by my fellow editor, Heidi Poon.

'Citizenship is a contested concept.' This is often said and is exemplified by the contributions to this book. Is a good citizen someone who contributes to social cohesion by conforming to the norms of that society, or someone who contributes to its development by being critical of how the society operates? Is citizenship a status or a call to action? Are citizens closely embedded in the culture of their community or do they stand somewhat apart from it, in a desire to be respectful of other cultures? Can citizenship be characterised by a set of general principles that govern human relations in any corporate or social setting or does it strike at the heart of the particularities of human experience? How closely is it tied to a particular political culture and can it, or should it, be divorced from the gutsy challenges of political action? How should it be taught? Is it a stand-alone subject or something which pervades the whole curriculum and the ethos of the school itself? And are these rigid distinctions or do mature citizens straddle all these perspectives?

At the heart of this debate are themes that have deep theological resonances. We are immediately challenged by questions about what it is to be human. By its nature, citizenship locates these challenges in the quality of the relationships we have with other people, in how we love our neighbour, or discharge our social responsibilities. How far does our respect for the dignity of our fellow citizens go? Does it extend to setting aside values and principles that go deep in our own faith tradition, in order to give our neighbour the cultural space to live according to a different, and perhaps incompatible, set of principles? As we seek the peace of the city, do we allow our values to be compromised in the service of that peace, or is peace valid only when it is based on a justice that transcends particular cultural principles? As we enter into dialogue with others about issues that matter deeply to us and that shape the character of our community, is it necessary for our language to lose the rich sonorities of centuries of reflection and be thinned into a superficial discourse that seems inadequate for its task? Or does the cultural exchange that citizens participate in enrich the traditions to which they belong?

Throughout the discussions in this book lurks the spectre of a humanity that is reduced to procedure and management and numerical control. We are challenged to preserve the throbbing reality of persons who hope and love and are vulnerable in the face of systems of civic control that promise respect but too often deliver an environment that fails to connect with people's needs and aspirations. The political climate of the early twenty-first century is nervous about people's passions, especially when expressed in the context of a particular faith. But how successful will the strategy be of denying these passions in the name of a citizenship that is driven only by skills and procedural accountability?

Citizenship is a hot topic in today's Britain. HM Government is concerned at the signs of disaffection in certain sectors of the community and sees an enhanced attention to the 'common bond' of citizenship as an important element in developing better social cohesion.[2] They see the challenge as that of renewing a shared sense of belonging and working to engage better with those who do not share it. Proposals for a national day and citizenship ceremonies are part of a portfolio of suggestions for how this might be achieved, which also includes an emphasis on active participation in society.

Yet that report's supportive research reveals that citizens of Britain differ in how they construct their identity and in how they express their citizenship.[3] The chapter in this volume by Paterson and Bond reports an interaction between perspectives on the civic element in education and perceived national identity on the part of academics with Scottish and English backgrounds.

More significantly for the purposes of this volume, the formal approaches to education for citizenship in Scotland and in England differ in important respects. For a start, England has a national curriculum, while Scotland does not, and citizenship can be a distinct subject within that curriculum. In 1999, the Scottish Consultative Council on the curriculum instigated a review of education for citizenship, which reported in 2002. It took the position that education for citizenship should be a key overarching purpose of the whole curriculum, preparing young people for thoughtful and responsible participation in political, economic and social life. Its model citizen was active and critical of his or her society, and schools were challenged to develop an ethos in which these capacities could be nurtured. Pamela Munn chaired the review group and she assesses the progress of these recommendations in her chapter in this book.

The idea that citizens should be agents of conformity dies hard, even in a context that encourages a more dissenting perspective, as Munn found, where schools reported better compliance and less disruption as a consequence of highlighting citizenship. David Carr goes back to the sources of modern approaches to citizenship, to be found in the reflections of seventeenth- and eighteenth-century philosophers on how to achieve social cohesion. The threats to this cohesion were identified in pre-civil modes of association and the recommendation was that these normative attachments and loyalties should be replaced with a rationally negotiated social contract. Reasoning based on evidence supplanted earlier religious forms of understanding but also courted the danger of discarding important insights from literature and the arts. Carr discusses MacIntyre's approach of identifying narrative as a source of moral conduct and affirms the value of the humanities as a training ground for citizenship. According to Paterson and Bond, this used to be the Scottish approach, seeing the engagement with a cultural tradition as the best preparation for citizenship.

To talk about preparing for citizenship is to take a position on the status of children as citizens. Kathleen Marshall is the Scottish Commissioner for Children and Young People and her chapter explores the question of whether children have to grow into being citizens or whether they are already citizens but their capacity for action still needs some development. Arguing from within the framework of the UN Convention on the Rights of the Child, she makes the case for regarding children as citizens who need to be helped to be active as such. She sees citizenship as the capacity to influence the forces that impact on your life and so the process of involving children in making decisions that affect their life is an exercise in citizenship. She outlines ways in which this process can be facilitated, so challenging the view that citizenship is a status that one enters at adulthood, in the context of a particular political tradition.

Whether children are learning to exercise their rights for participation in decisions that affect them, or preparing to become citizens, it does not happen without thought and careful training, according to Duncan Forrester. He makes a surprising connection between the tough love of a God who loves us enough to bother about us, and the discipline brought by a nanny into the lives of unruly children. For Forrester, the stakes are high, no less than proper solidarity and true justice. And he challenges the Church with the proposal that the Church is called to be a school of citizenship, rich with imaginative ways of loving and of doing justice, marked by generosity and gentle welcome in a harsh and suspicious world.

Paying attention to the environment in which citizens grow is a challenge for the whole community. Ian Martin calls this the contingent approach to citizenship. For Martin, citizens are political animals and so citizenship education is a matter of learning for democracy. He identifies several skills that this entails – taking sides, acting in solidarity, taking risks, developing political literacy, working at the grassroots, listening to dissenting voices, cultivating awkwardness, educating for social change, exploring alternatives and exposing the power of language.

Several of these skills are recruited by the citizens that are the focus of Eurig Scandrett's chapter. His concern is with environmental justice, an issue that requires an extended concept of citizenship. His citizen reaches beyond the horizon of a territorial nation state to being a citizen of the earth, with all its interconnected ecological relations. He develops the parable of the Good Samaritan to identify the kind of responsibility that we owe to our fellow citizen through this global lens, a responsibility that rests on the actual harm that our actions do to others. This is a system of asymmetric relations, shaped by the injustices of globalisation and of class. Scandrett has developed a programme called Agents for Environmental Justice which builds on people's lived experiences till they identify global issues on which they campaign, so combining political practice with theoretical analysis.

Taking risks is one of the skills that Martin lists as characteristic of learning for democracy, the risk of going beyond the comforts of familiar experience and discovering new horizons. This is an essential component of the working practice of the scientist and Wilson Poon argues that today's citizen needs to be able to think about science and technology, to understand the risks that are an irreducible feature of the technological process. The expectations laid on scientists often betray a misunderstanding of how scientific knowledge becomes established – yet being clear about this ought to be within the competence of citizens in the high-tech world we live in today.

Thinking about developments in biological science poses new challenges to our citizens and Rodney Taylor outlines the kinds of dilemmas to be met in this area and how citizens can be prepared to face them. There are four well-established principles of bioethics – autonomy, justice, beneficence and nonmaleficence – and students can be trained to learn them and apply them to particular cases. However, Taylor exposes the aridity of this approach based on principles and argues for a more substantive approach that captures the richness of human learning, as people struggle to be truly human.

Bringing the resources of traditional cultural communities directly into the ambit of education for citizenship most obviously happens in the interaction between religious education and citizenship education. Mark Halstead explores this engagement within the context of the English educational system. At first blush, these two subjects ought to reinforce each other – both dealing with attitudes and values, community involvement, developing skills in critical reflection and learning about diversity and pluralism. Yet the subjects are, rightly, taught in distinctive ways and the differences matter. One subject considers the spiritual response of loving one's neighbour, the other the civic responsibility towards one's fellow citizen. In the sensitive area of cultural diversity, religious studies might celebrate that diversity, while a particular attitude to citizenship would see this as something only to tolerate.

Donald Smith's chapter takes culture and the arts as the arena of citizenship education and outlines the history of public support of the arts in Scotland and attitudes towards its civic purpose. He reveals an interesting trail of differing evaluations of the contribution the arts can make to various dimensions of public worth – economic, social and educational – and shows how the purely aesthetic purpose of the arts is often curiously downplayed. Yet local culture and history provide an excellent soil in which to grow the kinds of critical understanding that are essential to the active citizen.

The practice of accounting would appear to be worlds away from the arts. Heidi Poon traces the way in which features of financial accounting have invaded society as a metaphor for responsibility and trustworthiness. Rather than trusting our fellow citizens, we put our trust in systems of auditing and regulation. These systems appear to be objective and impartial, yet their demands shape the practices of the professionals they regulate in ways that can be damaging. Moreover, there is a misunderstanding at the root of the metaphor, since accounting systems are not free of human agency and depend on human judgement themselves. Correcting the damage that this audit society can do to our understanding of human agency is an urgent challenge for those educating today's citizens.

The contributions to this volume come predominantly from a Scottish base but the issues that they address are of general significance. The first half of the book contains chapters that look at the nature of citizenship and how it might be nurtured. The remaining chapters focus on a particular area of experience and ask what qualities a citizen should develop in order to deal competently and responsibly with the decisions that need to be made in that area.

The book has had a long genesis but the questions posed within it are still fresh and current. May I thank all the contributors for their patience and commitment; the MB Reckitt Trust for its support; the University of Edinburgh for its hospitality throughout the process; and Saint Andrew Press for taking the initiative to publish *Growing Citizens*.

ALISON ELLIOT

Notes

1. Johnston R. McKay (ed.), *Netting Citizens* (Edinburgh: Saint Andrew Press, 2004).
2. Lord Goldsmith, 'Citizenship: Our Common Bond', www.justice.gov.uk/docs/citizenship-report-full.pdf (accessed 28 June 2008).
3. Anthony Heath and Jane Roberts, 'British Identity: its sources and possible implications for civic attitudes and behaviour', www.justice.gov.uk/docs/british-identity.pdf (accessed 28 June 2008).

Contributors

ROSS BOND, of the School of Social and Political Science in the University of Edinburgh, does research into nationalism and national identity; and Scottish society and politics.

DAVID CARR is Professor of Philosophy of Education at the Moray House School of Education, in the University of Edinburgh.

ALISON ELLIOT is Associate Director of the Centre for Theology and Public Issues in the School of Divinity in the University of Edinburgh, was Moderator of the General Assembly of the Church of Scotland and lectured in Developmental Psychology at the Universities of Edinburgh and Lancaster

DUNCAN B. FORRESTER is Emeritus Professor of Christian Ethics and Practical Theology and founder of the Centre for Theology and Public Issues at the University of Edinburgh.

J. MARK HALSTEAD is Professor of Education and Professional Development at the University of Huddersfield and Head of its Department of Community and International Education.

KATHLEEN MARSHALL is a specialist in child law and Scottish Commissioner for Children and Young People.

IAN MARTIN is Reader in Adult and Community Education at Moray House, University of Edinburgh.

PAMELA MUNN is Professor of Curriculum Research at the Moray House School of Education, University of Edinburgh, and was Chair of the Review Group on Education for Citizenship of the Scottish Consultative Council on the Curriculum.

LINDSAY PATERSON is Professor of Educational Policy at the University of Edinburgh.

HEIDI POON is Director of Tax in the Private Client Division at Morton Fraser, is a member of the Institute of Chartered Accountants of Scotland and the Chartered Institute of Taxation, London, and a judiciary member of the VAT and Duties Tribunals.

WILSON POON, of the Scottish Universities Physics Alliance, is Professor of Condensed Matter Physics in the School of Physics at the University of Edinburgh.

EURIG SCANDRETT lectures in Sociological Theory in Media, Communication and Sociology at the Queen Margaret University and was Head of Community Action at Friends of the Earth Scotland.

DONALD SMITH is Director of the Scottish Storytelling Centre, was Chair of the Scottish National Theatre Working Party and is Chair of the Literature Forum for Scotland.

RODNEY TAYLOR was a member of the ESRC Genomics Forum at the University of Edinburgh and is Assistant Professor of Theology at Hardin Simmons University, Abilene, Texas, USA.

Citizenship and the Cultural Roots of Civil Value

David Carr

The Roots of Modern Citizenship

The sources of modern concepts of citizenship may be traced to the attempts of seventeenth- and eighteenth-century contract theorists to explain the basis of social cohesion in the wake of human progression from pre-civil modes of association (the so-called state of nature) to civil society. The classic contract theorists diverge considerably in their accounts of the basic function and purpose of rules of civil order. For Hobbes, the purpose of such rules is to limit freedom in the interests of security (Hobbes 1968);[1] for Locke their function is precisely to safeguard individual liberty and rights from potential state interference (Locke 1966);[2] for Rousseau their ultimate point is to promote democratic social justice (Rousseau 1973).[3] Moreover, despite obvious tensions and contradictions between these accounts, aspects of all of them have informed the contemporary mainstream of liberal-democratic thought. Indeed, the basic liberal thesis of Locke and his chief political heir John Stuart Mill (1859),[4] that the purpose of law is to ensure liberty, is neatly combined with a wider principled regard for the common good derived from Rousseau and Kant in the more recently influential philosophy of John Rawls (1985, 1993)[5] – a theory that also acknowledges the Hobbesian concern that law should protect security.

This is not to deny that there are tensions between these views. For one thing, whereas a greater Lockian or Millian emphasis on liberty may incline towards less egalitarian or distributive social policies, a Rousseauian or Kantian concern with selfless autonomy is likely to lead to a greater political emphasis on common welfare over individual freedom. For present purposes, however, it is more important to notice what all these conceptions of civil order have in common – and I shall here consider two such features.

First, all these conceptions emphasise that any successful transition from the pre-civil state to full civil membership must involve some departure from erstwhile normative attachments and loyalties. For Hobbes, entry into civil society involves renouncing the liberties of the state of nature – not least the freedom of the strong to exploit the weak. On this view, the basis of civil law and order is to be no longer the arbitrary will of the local clan chief, but a universal sovereign law to which all are subject and which safeguards the rights of all. Again, for Locke and his liberal heirs, although the laws of civil society are partly designed to protect individual loyalties to traditional religious or other pre-civil values and identities, their purpose is primarily to preclude any external interference in the right of individuals to self-determination and free expression as such. Finally, although Rousseau recognised more clearly than most the dangers of social divisiveness and fragmentation consequent upon transition from his pre-lapsarian state of nature to the social free-for-all of more advanced civil societies, he did not regard a return to pre-civil loyalties and attachments as the way to break the chains he saw as binding his own divided society. Rather, his solution lay in educating modern citizens towards a higher association grounded in a philosophically abstract notion of justice as universal reciprocity.

In short, despite differences, all the classic contract theorists conceived modern citizens as sites of rights and duties that may not just override but actually estrange them from their pre-civil loyalties and attachments. The good liberal-democratic citizen is someone whose first allegiance is to the laws of civil (national or super-national) state rather than to any local religious or other cultural values, no matter how formative of identity such values might otherwise be.

The second notable common feature of these conceptions, however, is the highly abstract, formal or general character of the values and principles that are ultimately held to define or underpin civil membership. The commitments of civil citizens are not the 'thick' values of cultural inheritance or religious belief – though the extent to which the Judaeo-Christian tradition has influenced modern liberal-democratic thought can be acknowledged – but rather the 'thin' procedural principles of rationally negotiated social contract. The basic liberal-democratic principles of reciprocal respect and tolerance are precisely supposed to secure any and all necessary social cooperation between those of different cultural loyalties and faiths. Such cooperation has, of course, become a matter of pressing priority as economic and other migration has led to an unprecedented degree of cultural diversity and pluralism in modern liberal democracies. In short, the key task for modern liberal states, no less than for seventeenth- and eighteenth-century contract theorists, is that of educating citizens to regard local or traditional loyalties and attachments as significantly secondary to their commitments to the procedural values of modern civil society.

The Contemporary Problem of Education for Citizenship

The idea of citizenship as basically grounded in procedural values of openness, tolerance and respect for democratically established law has also informed recent policy proposals regarding citizenship education in Britain and elsewhere. To be sure, there are some differences of curricular approach between recent English and Scottish developments in this sphere: for example, whereas English developments, in the wake of the Crick report,[6] have aimed to give a more formal and explicit place to citizenship education as a national curriculum subject, recent Scottish documentation[7] (Learning and Teaching Scotland 2002) has focused more on cross-curricular possibilities, and the promotion of appropriate school ethos. Still, such strategic differences should not blind us to the extent to which these different initiatives have drawn on much the same basic tenets of modern liberal-democratic philosophy and theory in view of an essentially shared perception of the key issues and problems of contemporary citizenship.

What are these problems? We may divide them broadly into problems of social and educational deficit and excess.

The problems of deficit have both a practical and a theoretical dimension. The first, practical dimension concerns an allegedly widespread contemporary disengagement from public life and the political process: ordinary citizens seem increasingly reluctant to give up their own time to public or community service, and may often nowadays be too politically alienated even to vote in local and general elections. The academic or theoretical dimension of deficit, on the other hand, relates to an equally apparent widespread public ignorance about either the structure and processes of political democracy or the key global and local political issues of the day that may already be having an adverse impact on their own personal and private lives and interests.

The problems of excess are less manifest in what citizens are not doing, more in what they are doing – precisely in what appears to be a rise in anti-social, anomic and even nihilistic behaviour, perhaps most notably among the young. Such decline in public and private conduct is reflected in the dreary litany of criminal and/or irresponsible actions – apparent at all levels of society – that routinely disgrace the news of the day.

At this point, it might be noted that some have been drawn to trace both the vices of (anti)social excess and civic deficit to a common source in asocial and possessive individualism directly attributable to liberal-democratic concepts of human association. On this view, the modern political separation of the thin procedural values of citizenship from the thick values of pre-civil association may be regarded as a major cause of the contemporary climate of 'devil-take-the-hindmost' individualism.

Clearly, however, any such simplistic view of wholesale liberal individualist corruption of an original communitarian paradise of thicker normative character fails to do justice to the complexities of moral, social and political decline in our own and similar societies. To begin with, far from preaching selfish individualism over other-regarding association, modern liberal democratic theory advocates a wider and more inclusive view of such association – of precisely who should be considered one's neighbour. Likewise, it is far from obvious that the thick values of traditional community are or have always been conducive to the promotion of greater civic responsibility or socio-political order and justice. From this viewpoint, the causes of (anti)social excess and civic deficit in many western liberal-democratic societies are undoubtedly complex and not to be attributed to any single socio-cultural trend or tendency.

Liberal Democracy and the Sources of Moral Commitment

However, despite some popular tendency to associate liberalism with secularism, the nature and extent of any such association is controversial. First, although political liberalism may have entrained secularism in some contemporary – perhaps, especially, western European – polities, it has not done so in others: the United States, for example, seems to be a place of widespread religious loyalty and affiliation. Second, any claim that liberalism is inherently secular overlooks the fact that liberal theory had its very origins in a post-Reformation concern to defend freedom of individual *religious* conscience against any potentially tyrannical alliance of the state with this or that sectarian agenda. Hence, the familiar liberal idea (enshrined in the constitutional arrangements of some modern states) that the political apparatus of a democratic state should be secular – in short, neutral between different comprehensive theories of the good – does not mean that any liberal perspective would have to be secular (or atheistic). On the contrary, the idea that no serious normative perspectives are to be excluded from the liberal conversation about human destiny and flourishing, is absolutely integral to liberalism. It is noteworthy that in older liberal democracies – such as the United Kingdom – in which there has not been strict separation between religion and state, religious education has had a protected place and status in the school curriculum.

Despite this, some historical association of liberal theory with – if not quite secularism – then at least a certain scepticism regarding the religious and other sources of local cultural values is hard to gainsay. The core liberal commitment is to free and open rational enquiry, and for that to be rational it must be evidence-based. Thus, any mainstream liberal epistemology would have to be largely empiricist. Hence, it is no accident that liberal theory – in the classical Millian statement of the doctrine – is wedded to the essentially naturalist and verificationist ethics of utility. Moreover, although such twentieth-century liberal theorists as John Rawls have drawn more on the non-empiricist ethics of Kant than upon utilitarianism, Kant's categorical imperatives have here been purged of their transcendental associations in favour of a much more naturalistic contractual interpretation – whereby the basic rules of moral law are now no longer the legislations of non-empirical noumenal selves, more the formal conditions of any viable moral and civil order. Kantian reasons of reciprocal regard can be given for why everyone should tell the truth or keep their promises, but no such reasons can be given for holding that Jesus loves us or that one's fate is the will of Allah. Although no one is to be denied freedom to profess such beliefs, they could not be rationally adopted as universally agreeable grounds for moral and civil association. It is also worth noting that such contemporary liberal interpretations of Kant are quite in line with this philosopher's own thought. Kant explicitly held that the normative deliverances of practical reason were non-empirical but rational. Although his own religious commitment cannot be doubted, he also argued that the claims of faith could not be supported by reason and took great pains to refute traditional arguments for the existence of God.

It is also worth noting, however, that Kant's autonomous moral reason and judgement is insulated not only from empirical fact and religious faith but also from the realms of aesthetic experience and artistic appreciation. Just as Kant's ethics denies the relevance of empirical knowledge or religious claims to moral enquiry, so the time-honoured contribution of literature and the arts to the cultivation of moral and spiritual understanding and sensibility is disavowed by Kant's ethical and aesthetic theories. The idea that poetry and other forms of fictional literature can be important sources of normative understanding is clearly central to Aristotle's *Poetics* (in McKeon 1941)[8] as well as generally consistent with his ethics of virtue. It is therefore unsurprising that this idea has received more sympathetic treatment in the recent neo-Aristotelian revival of virtue ethics – not least in the work of the influential moral and social theorist Alasdair MacIntyre (1981).[9]

MacIntyre argues that the key to understanding agency in general and/or moral conduct in particular is the idea of *narrative*. In this regard, he denies the possibility of understanding human identity and action in the causal terms of natural or social science. The accounts of human life and conduct offered by reductive social and behavioural science can shed no meaningful light on personal identity and agency – precisely to the extent that they ignore or deny the teleological or narrative dimensions of such inherently purposive agency. Hence, understanding self and identity is not a matter of establishing physical or psychological criteria of continuity, but of understanding the roles occupied by agents in more or less rational narratives that others tell about them or which they tell about themselves.

The notion that humans cannot understand themselves as other than agents in narratives – as actors, as it were, in the dramas of life – is an appealing one for those who believe in the general significance of stories for moral, spiritual and other self-understanding. It is clearly of the first importance to MacIntyre, for whom the traditions that he wishes to uphold as integral to any significant sense of human identity or personhood – namely religious, spiritual, moral and artistic traditions – are precisely composed of narratives or stories in this sense.

Narratives as Potential Sources of Universal Value

In short, a significant feature of MacIntyre's work is that it serves to reaffirm the personally and morally formative significance and value of story and narrative that seems to have been downplayed in later developments of modern political and social liberalism. For while it should be admitted that such nineteenth-century architects of liberalism as Matthew Arnold (see Gribble 1967)[10] regarded the great literary traditions as central to a liberal education – conceived as initiation into 'the best that has been thought and said' – it would appear that the twentieth-century liberal separation of the procedural values of political association from the substantial values of local cultural narrative is linked to a certain agnosticism regarding such local cultural productions. Modern liberalism is implicated in an enlightenment rationalism according to which empirical science would seem to be the only reliable touchstone of genuine human knowledge. In this light, mainstream liberalism has largely consigned the non-empirical beliefs and values of grand cultural narratives to the realm of personal or local taste or commitment: since such narratives cannot be held to provide any non-controversial basis for civil association they can only be irrelevant to the promotion of citizenship in a liberal polity.

If MacIntyre is right, however, modern political liberalism may be mistaken not only about the epistemic status of the stories and narratives of cultural inheritance, but also about the educational foundations of liberal polity and citizenship. In short, it may be mistaken not only to restrict genuine knowledge to empirical science, but also to suppose that the grand myths and narratives of past and present cultures and civilisations, not to mention their literary modes of expression and communication, can make little or no substantial contribution to the cultivation of civil and civilised sensibility. In this light, there might seem to be no compelling reason why citizenship education would have to involve procedural disengagement of individuals from their traditional religious, artistic and other cultural attachments, if not some case for supposing that this is where the moral roots of citizenship might actually be found.

But this claim is not unproblematic. The potential downside of MacIntyre's affirmation of the teleological structures of narrative and story as important forms of self-understanding turns on his non-realist or social constructivist reading of both moral purpose and virtue which seems to undermine the status of such narratives and stories as *objective* forms of knowledge and understanding. As already noticed, MacIntyre regards moral virtues, and the cultural narratives that serve to define such virtues, as conditioned all the way down by local socio-cultural interest and concerns. On the basis of an essentially non-realist moral epistemology, MacIntyre is drawn to conclude that the heroic virtues of Homeric antiquity – as defined precisely by the narratives of the *Iliad* and *Odyssey* – cannot be properly comprehended or evaluated from other rival moral and cultural perspectives, not least any that might be readily available to the citizens of present-day liberal democracies. On this view, if a virtue is a particular ordering of moral sensibility, then we cannot from any contemporary perspective hope to gain much insight into the perspectives and/or experiences of a Paris, Helen, Menelaus, Agamemnon, Odysseus, Hector or Achilles, or the moral ideals and values according to which they lived. It might also seem to follow from this that there could be little contemporary point in attempting to read the *Odyssey* or *Iliad* – at least for any significant moral educational purpose. Presumably the same would apply to reading such religious texts and narratives as Genesis or Exodus, the *Mahabharata*, the Koran or the New Testament Gospels and Epistles.

Worse yet, such radical epistemic constructivism draws MacIntyre perilously close to the political anti-liberal agenda of contemporary social and political communitarians. Although the communitarian case against liberalism is too complex for present detailed exploration, communitarians generally allege that the procedural universals of liberal association are too thin and insubstantial to sustain social cohesion and that any genuine solidarity may be secured only by subscription to normative perspectives or narratives expressive of the more particular social, economic, territorial and other interests of local community. On this view, it is not just that local narratives enshrine concepts of virtue and value that must be virtually incomprehensible from rival cultural perspectives, but that it is central to the purpose(s) of such narratives to cultivate some such sense of local loyalty and common cause. The trouble now, however, is that the communitarian defence of cultural narratives in terms of their role in the affirmation of local interests and agendas seems no more conducive to the vindication of their general educational significance than liberal agnosticism.

However, apart from the philosophically paradoxical nature of all such forms of incommensurabilism and/or relativism – that such theses, if true, could hardly even be stated – claims of this kind seem intuitively implausible from more commonsense moral and educational perspectives. Indeed, MacIntyre's historicist account of virtue seems to depart from both the Aristotelian virtue ethical mainstream and ordinary moral understanding. First, although the Aristotelian view emphasises that virtuous agency needs to be adapted to context – and that contexts of virtue are prone to some normative diversity – it also takes a quite naturalistic view of the inclinations, passions and feelings that it is the prime function of virtuous principles and judgements to regulate, and it seems to be no part of the Aristotelian view that we cannot judge, even cross-culturally, between better and worse orderings of such natural dispositions. Second, on some such more commonsense virtue ethical perspective, it seems fairly clear that the discourse of virtue does provide a fairly reliable cross-cultural currency of moral evaluation and that we can and do successfully commend those of other cultures for their honesty, integrity, fairness, self-control, courage and compassion – or blame them for their duplicity, cowardice or cruelty – even where we do not share their moral values or beliefs, or even where we find such values and beliefs barely comprehensible. By these same tokens, however, it is no less implausible to suppose that we can have nothing to gain morally or otherwise educationally from reading the literary works of other times and places that explore the complexities of human character and virtue. On the contrary, apart from the fact that the cultures of present-day western liberal democracy are directly heir to those of classical antiquity – that we can hardly comprehend contemporary western culture without reference to ancient Greek and Roman sources – one reason for regarding acquaintance with past historical and wider world literature as an educational *sine qua non* is that it has the potential to broaden human moral and other horizons in just this way. To be sure, it is probably true that as modern liberal-democrats (or whatever) we can hardly be expected to *share* the moral values and perspectives of a Priam, Clytemnestra or Antigone: but the great Greek dramas that feature such characters continue to be compelling precisely for what they can teach us, not just about alien cultural values, but objectively about human nature.

Hence, if the liberal reduction to subjective taste of the time-honoured cultural narratives of humankind appears ill-judged, then their assimilation by communitarians to local social interests may seem hardly less so. Despite any and all abuses to which the teaching of the western literary canon may sometimes have been subject, we cannot plausibly suppose that it has invariably, if ever, been the primary educational aim of teaching Shakespeare to promote the superiority of British culture over others. The folly and ignorance of interpreting *The Merchant of Venice* as a racist tract, for example, hardly needs demonstrating to any reasonably educated person: on the contrary, Shakespeare's drama precisely holds up a mirror to those prejudices of our own cultural inheritance that have continued to yield such a bitter harvest down to our own times. Indeed, the lessons of truly great literature are precisely *universal* – as the conspicuous interest in Shakespeare of a very great contemporary Japanese film director (Kurosawa) bears sufficient witness. The truth about the great narratives of cultural invention is that they are the most basic resource of human normative enquiry, in default of which it is hard to see how any serious interrogation of human values might ever get started. Moreover, it is also evident that some of these great sources of normative reflection and enquiry – from Dante's *Divine Comedy*, Bunyan's *Pilgrim's Progress* and Milton's *Paradise Lost* to Thomas Mann's *Joseph and his Brothers*, Hermann Hesse's *Siddhartha*, Salman Rushdie's *Satanic Verses* and Philip Pullman's *His Dark Materials* – have drawn in various ways upon the great religious narratives of Buddhism, Islam and (particularly) the Christian Bible, and that it is hardly possible to profess an educated understanding of such landmarks of literary heritage without substantial acquaintance with the religious narratives by which they have been inspired (albeit from sometimes critical perspectives).

Religion, Humanities and Citizenship Education

But there is the rub. For the great religious narratives have not only or primarily attracted attention as important literary sources of or stimuli to moral reflection, but have also been regarded as direct accounts or expressions of the precise word of (some) God or his prophets. It is on this ground that such narratives have traditionally formed the basis of religious education – or even schooling as such – in theocracies or strongly religiously defined cultures, and have been regarded with suspicion or hostility from more sceptical secular liberal perspectives on such revelation, perhaps, *inter alia*, as potential sources of social division. Indeed, such apparently iconoclastic works as Salman Rushdie's *Satanic Verses* and Philip Pullman's *His Dark Materials* have attracted the odium and censure of the faithful, precisely because they have been considered subversive of divinely revealed truth. In short, while such narratives are subject to secular liberal suspicion precisely because they seem to be little more than fictions, the fundamentalism of some faith school contexts refuses to tolerate any other narratives (such as, for one obvious example, Darwin's *Origin of Species*) insofar as they appear to contradict the inviolable sacred texts.

There can also be no doubt that these general views of the status of religious narrative – that it contains all (final) truth or no (even provisional) truth – have had a deeply compromising and divisive effect on contemporary philosophy of religious education. On this way of thinking, the great stories of religious cultural inheritance (which is invariably also modern secular inheritance) have been caught between the 'rock' of a narrow confessional approach in contexts approaching religious indoctrination, and the 'hard place' of a watered-down liberal pluralist religious education usually focused on the promotion of intercultural knowledge and understanding of an often fairly superficial anthropological or sociological character. At first sight, it might seem plainly reasonable to suppose that traditional confessional induction into some particular religious faith is no longer an option for common schools in contemporary (British and other) culturally plural contexts. But it is also arguable that neither of these opposed perspectives on religious narrative and education – neither blind faith in literal truth nor sceptical disengagement from the normative potential of religious story – can do adequate justice to the influence of religious narratives on western and other cultural history and on the various literary traditions that have shaped even contemporary secular educational perspectives and sensibilities. Moreover, in so failing, both may neglect the significant contribution of religious understanding and understanding of religion to educated citizenship.

The significance of some such religious and theological contribution to any substantial civil and civic sensibility is appreciated in a paper on citizenship by Professor Richard Pring. For Pring, the potential for substantial and meaningful citizenship education is already there in the central place accorded by many traditional curricula to the study of what he calls the 'humanities', and he mourns the passing of explicit modern attempts to develop humanities education after the fashion, for example, of Lawrence Stenhouse's *Humanities Curriculum Project* (Stenhouse et al. 1970).[11] Of the humanities in general, Pring says:

> The humanities, therefore – the poetry, the novels, the dance, the media presentations, the arts, the historical accounts, the social interpretation, the theological analysis – were, as it were, the text, the touchstone, the objects through which emerged the transaction between teacher and learner, and between the learners themselves as they examined critically those issues of supreme personal, social and political importance: sexual relations, social justice, the use of violence, the respect (or disrespect) for authority, racism and so on. (Pring 1999, p. 83)[12]

In short, for Pring, religion and theology would appear to make best sense as part of a general humanities programme in which they feature along with history, literature and the arts as modes of enquiry through which humans have tried to understand themselves, their place in the world and their relations with others. If MacIntyre is right, that the key mode of human self-understanding is precisely the narratival form of religion, history and literature, it is therefore hardly surprising that traditional cultures have widely approached education through the telling of stories. Some stories, of course, such as fairy tales, are meant to be eventually outgrown – although the best of such stories may also contain lasting insights into the human condition (as the works of Marina Warner (1995, 2000, 2002), Angela Carter (2005) and others have demonstrated).[13] Others, however, have been rightly considered more adult fare and precisely as sources of wisdom regarding the grounds of worthwhile attachment; many such stories are enshrined in the great artistic and other cultural narratives – including religious narratives – of humankind. Hence, in a world of contemporary liberal or other scepticism regarding the epistemic or normative status and value of such stories – where they may be regarded as little more than entertaining postmodern fictions, and where the *Mahabharata*, *Paradise Lost* or *Macbeth* may be valued no more highly than *Peyton Place* or *Goldfinger* – the young may well lie under the shadow of a cultural disinheritance that does indeed constitute a genuine threat to any real quality of civilised citizenship.

Of course, serious engagement with such narratives may well lead to the formation of particular loyalties, attachments and commitments, some of which may be religious or spiritual. However, as I have argued more fully elsewhere (Carr 1996),[14] this does not mean that such values would need to be in any way inconsistent with the general liberal injunction to treat everyone – stranger no less than friend – as our neighbour in some spirit of universal justice: indeed, that imperative probably owes much, if not everything, to its roots in perhaps the greatest western religious story ever told. But the more general lesson for present consideration is that it is hard if not impossible to internalise the liberal injunction to universal respect in the absence of some opportunity and capacity for serious contemplation of the profound issues of human value and purpose for which the major cultural narratives of Pring's humanities have always provided a key educational inspiration and resource.

Notes

1. T. Hobbes, *Leviathan* (Harmondsworth: Penguin, 1968).
2. J. Locke, *Two Treatises of Civil Government* (London: Dent Everyman, 1966).
3. J.-J. Rousseau, *The Social Contract and other Discourses* (London: Dent, 1973).
4. J. S. Mill, *On Liberty* (1859), in M. Warnock (ed.), *Utilitarianism* (London: Collins, the Fontana Library, 1970).
5. J. Rawls, *A Theory of Justice* (Cambridge: Harvard University Press, 1985); J. Rawls, *Political Liberalism* (New York: Columbia University Press, 1993).
6. B. Crick, *Education for Citizenship and the Teaching of Democracy in Schools: Final Report of the Advisory Group on Citizenship* (London: Qualifications and Curriculum Authority, 1998).
7. Learning and Teaching Scotland, *Education for Citizenship in Scotland: a paper for discussion and development* (Dundee and Glasgow: LTS, 2002).
8. Aristotle, *Poetics*, in R. McKean, *The Basic Works of Aristotle* (New York: Random House, 1941).
9. A. C. MacIntyre, *After Virtue* (Notre Dame: Notre Dame Press, 1981).
10. J. Gribble, *Matthew Arnold* (London: Collier Macmillan Educational Thinkers Series, 1967).
11. L. Stenhouse, et al., *The Humanities Project: an introduction* (London: Heinemann, 1970).
12. R. Pring, 'Political Education: relevance of the humanities', *Oxford Review of Education* 25, 1 & 2 (1999), pp. 71–87.
13. M. Warner, *From the Beast to the Blonde: on fairy tales and their tellers* (London: Vintage, 1995); M. Warner, *No Go the Bogeyman* (London: Vintage, 2000); M. Warner, *Fantastic Metamorphoses: other worlds* (Oxford: Oxford University Press, 2002); A. Carter, *Angela Carter's Book of Fairy Tales* (London: Virago Press, 2005).

14. D. Carr, 'The Moral Roots of Citizenship: towards a virtue ethical reconciliation of rights and character for effective citizenship', *Journal of Moral Education*, Special Issue on Citizenship 35, 4 (1996), forthcoming.

Citizenship and the Just Society

Duncan B. Forrester

When we speak about citizens we are affirming (contra Margaret Thatcher) that society exists, and that it is not simply a group of independent individuals accidentally side by side, or a collection of people locked together in controversy and conflict, without shared interests or ties of altruism. John Paul II puts it thus:

> If the promotion of the self is understood in terms of absolute autonomy, people inevitably reach the point of rejecting one another. Everyone else is considered an enemy from whom one has to defend oneself. Thus society becomes a mass of individuals placed side by side, but without any mutual bonds. Each one wishes to assert himself independently of the other and in fact intends to make his own interests prevail.[1]

Citizens, on the other hand, belong to a *community* of people, bound together by links of accountability and responsibility for and to one another. They have claims on one another, and rights and duties in relation to one another. The way these links are organised and expressed determines whether a society is just or unjust, decent or oppressive. Citizenship is thus a specific way of speaking about solidarity. Citizens are not just members of a community, they are also responsible for the kind of community in which they live.

Active Citizenship

When we speak about *citizens* rather than *subjects* we are implying that citizens do not simply receive and obey orders from above. They participate in the life of the community; they cooperate with others; they share in decision-making; they contribute to the life of the community. Aristotle spoke of human beings as political animals by nature; in other words, the proper life for human beings was, he argued, one in which citizens shared freely in decision-making and in responsibility for one another. Less than that was not a fully human way of living. And it is still true that a healthy, just society has an active, participatory citizenry who fulfil their duties just as much as they claim their rights.

A society in which people participate in decision-making and actually attend to one another and the needs of the other is not easy to achieve. Even in democracies there is often, for various reasons, a low level of participation. There is a lot of paternalism in politics. Parties and ideologies of Left and of Right often suggest that a small group of intellectuals or politicians is more capable of taking decisions about what is good and just for others without consulting the citizens. But only the wearer of the shoe knows where it really pinches. The Roman Catholic principle of 'subsidiarity' suggests that decisions and decision-making should take place as close to the grassroots as possible. From a different angle, liberation theology urges that we need to learn from the poor and from the Bible what justice means; we cannot decide in advance what justice is for a particular community in a specific situation, and then implement it. Citizens are entitled to have a say about decisions which affect them.

Dependency[2]

Citizens are often assumed to be *independent* people. Dependency is said to be an inferior way of life to that of the citizen. But dependency, of course, is a natural part of the human lifecycle, and some people for a variety of reasons, sometimes good and sometimes bad, are highly dependent on others throughout their lives. Children are properly dependent on their parents; confused elderly people are dependent on their carers; when we are sick we learn how dependent we are on the skills of doctors and nurses; married couples have a proper dependence on one another. We all need to learn how to be dependent, and how to deal properly with people who are dependent on us. And all of us are dependent on others for countless things that make life possible and pleasant. Christians know that it is proper for us to be dependent on God, and that a healthy society is one in which there is much interdependence, a rich, vibrant pattern of dependency and support.

But there is another kind of dependency which demeans, and excludes and marginalises dependent people, making it hard for them to return to a fuller involvement in the life of the community. And any community that humiliates or demeans some of its citizens is not a decent or just society. A just society, on the other hand, affirms the worth of each of its citizens, and does not shame them.

The British welfare system as established in the 1940s has been accused, from Right and from Left, of encouraging a passive attitude towards welfare provision, launching multitudes of people into a harmful and degrading dependency, and locking people into a poverty trap. People such as Frank Field and Michael Ignatieff argue that welfare is not simply a passive entitlement of citizenship, but citizens have an active duty to seek the welfare of the whole community, and to take as much responsibility as possible for their own welfare and that of their families. But in a just society it is also necessary that state and voluntary agencies should provide welfare that does not demean or demoralise, but affirms the value of each citizen.

Older welfare systems, with their specious distinction between the 'deserving' and the 'undeserving' poor, and their readiness to blame the poor and the weak for their condition, systematically degraded and humiliated the poor in workhouses and other forms of 'relief'. Rather than going back to that, we must seek a welfare system which encourages the active participation of citizens at every point and discourages harmful forms of dependency.[3]

Citizens' Rights

Citizens are assumed to be equal to one another, particularly in the rights they possess. T. H. Marshall famously saw three levels or stages of citizenship rights.[4]

- First, there are the civil rights that we so often today take for granted – freedom of speech and expression, assembly, to a fair trial, etc. Here the stress is on equality before the law. Where the civil rights of a group of citizens are not effectively guaranteed, say by a defective system of criminal justice or racist policing, that group's full citizenship is being denied.
- Next come the political rights – the right to share in political power and decision-making through the vote, and so forth; democratic rights, in short. In practice, many of them are still in dispute today, in Britain.
- Finally come the social rights that are still vigorously contested in our society – the right to education, to welfare, to share to the full in the life of the society as a civilised being and a citizen.

It has been strongly and convincingly argued that those who do not possess effective social rights are second-class citizens, not able effectively to exercise their civil and political rights. In practice they are not equal before the law, and their political influence is negligible, partly because although they have the vote they lack influence, and have difficulty articulating their political concerns. It is also true that because the poor in Britain are an electoral minority, at election time none of the parties thinks them particularly important. Thus the poor, although possessing the vote and civil rights, are often marginalised and become an 'underclass', alienated and excluded from the mainstream.

Exclusion

Who are citizens? It is well known that in the cities of the ancient world and in the Roman Empire a small minority of males were the citizens. Citizenship was a special honour and privilege, as Paul the Apostle recognised when he claimed the exemptions and the privileged treatment to which only a Roman citizen was entitled. In the Greek city states women, slaves and aliens were all excluded from the privileges and responsibilities of citizenship. Their role was to provide the small minority of male citizens with the leisure and comfort required for the exercise of their duties as citizens! Ancient societies on the whole were not democratic and participative in the modern sense of these terms.

Democratic participation is still an issue in many countries, including Britain. Women, ethnic minorities and the poor are far from having the same access to power or control over their destiny as the more prosperous male white sectors of society. Nor do such groups find it easy to contribute to the flourishing of society. Minority groups need to be given a voice. A major concern today is the low level of involvement in the electoral process on the part of young people. Many of them just do not see the point of voting, and regard the political system as being remote from their concerns and unwilling to take their opinions into account.

The same issues of justice arise in relation to ethnic minorities. Although they have the vote and formal civil rights, the danger of marginalising ethnic and religious minorities to the point where they do not enjoy the equal protection of the law, or equal access to power and influence must be continually monitored. How just is a Britain in which so many black Britons walk in fear and Muslim communities are demonised?

Then there are the groups who are technically citizens, but are unable for one reason or another to play an active citizen's role in society. One thinks here of children, of the confused elderly, of people with severe learning difficulties, for example. It is important that such people are accorded the dignity of citizens, and are encouraged to play as active a role in the community as possible. Help with problems of mobility and access for people with physical difficulties is a matter of justice rather than pity or charity. And such people bring special gifts to the flourishing of a just and decent community.

Then there are people whose citizenship is elsewhere; although they live in a country they do not possess citizenship in the technical sense. There are, for example, refugees, seeking asylum from persecution, torture or hardship elsewhere. Such non-citizens may not be given the vote or incorporated within the political system, but it is important that they are treated with dignity and respect. A society is unjust if it treats a group of people who live in its territory unjustly, however well it treats its own citizens. The treatment of refugees and asylum seekers in Britain today is one of the great issues of social justice that we face.

Citizens of Heaven

Christians might wish to suggest that we already have some experience of a broader, global citizenship, for 'our true citizenship is in heaven'. We can broaden the understanding of citizenship somewhat in the way the Bible broadens the notion of the neighbour.

We read in the New Testament that 'We are citizens of heaven' (Philippians 3:20) and this makes us fellow-citizens with the saints of every clime and age and nation. This great fact relativises our earthly citizenship, and links us by ties of accountability and responsibility to people of many lands and cultures and generations as well as to our own fellow citizens. The Church is called to be the gathering of those on earth who believe that their true citizenship is in heaven, and that this great fact should shape their attitudes and behaviour fundamentally. The metaphysical poet, John Donne, put it thus:

> The Church is Catholike, universal, so are all her Actions; All that she does, belongs to all, when she baptizes a child, that action concerns mee; for that child is thereby connected to that Head which is my Head too, and engraffed into that body, whereof I am a member. And when she buries a (Hu)man, that action concerns me; all (hu)mankind is of one Author, and is one volume.[5]

Thus, in the earthly city Christians are 'resident aliens' who have a larger citizenship in the City of God. This does not at all mean that Christians are not concerned for the justice of the earthly city. We do not find justice for ourselves in a ghetto, accepting no responsibility for the wider world. We learn through our citizenship of the City of God something of what God's justice is, the justice we are to seek first if all things are to be given to us. We measure the justice of the earthly city against the justice of the City of God. We learn to be accountable to our 'fellow citizens' around the world.

The City of God in which we are all citizens is in principle a universal society in which all limited associations of state, class or race are overcome. Augustine emphasises the importance of justice. Without it, he claims, a state becomes demonic; and the justice of nations – their behaviour and their policies – must be measured against the loving justice of the reign of God.

Our experience as citizens of heaven, citizens of the City of God, should give us clues as to how to behave in modern globalised society. We are responsible for one another, accountable to one another. The needy stranger at the other side of the world has a claim upon us. Christians should be at the forefront of movements seeking economic and political justice in a world with such extreme inequalities of wealth and power.

Citizens as Neighbours

The primary sense of the word 'neighbour' is someone who lives near one, in the same neighbourhood. This is probably someone very like oneself, for birds of a feather flock together. In a South Indian village the Dalits (who used to be called Untouchables) still commonly live apart from the main village in their own *cheri*, and are not allowed to use the same wells or facilities as the caste people. They are regarded as different, lowly, despised; the caste people feel that they can treat them in a quite different way from their own kind, their neighbours. In the old days in the west, slaves and servants, even if they lived in the master's house, were seldom if ever treated as neighbours; they did not belong, they were different, they might support the life of the neighbourhood, but they were not part of it.

Nor is it much different with us in Britain. Our cities are surrounded with peripheral housing estates which are alien worlds to most people in the middle-class residential areas. Ignorance of this sort obstructs the development of neighbourly community and of justice.

Neighbours in the basic sense belong to a face-to-face community; they know one another. Neighbours may squabble, but they tend to stand shoulder-to-shoulder against any outside threat or challenge. And neighbours often care for one another in warm and wonderful ways. There are recognised standards of good neighbourliness which everyone knows, even if we often fail to live up to them. Neighbours have responsibilities to one another; neighbours belong together; they are interdependent; they ought to be able to rely on one another.

When the Bible enjoins us to love our neighbour, or to do good to our neighbour, it is often the natural neighbour, someone like us, who is in question first of all. But already in the Old Testament there is a significant extension of the meaning of the neighbour. In Leviticus 19:18, for instance, there is an injunction to love the neighbour, and the context makes it abundantly clear that it is a person just like us, the child of our own people, who is in question. But towards the close of the same chapter (vv. 33–4), the Israelites are enjoined to do something far more difficult: to love the strangers in their midst, the people who are different.

The marginalised people, that means, are to be loved and accepted as if they were in fact physical neighbours; excluded people are to be incorporated into the moral community of Israel and treated as neighbours. The stranger is to be treated as a neighbour, and this for two specific reasons: the Israelite memory of having themselves been slaves in Egypt has – or ought to have – taught them the bitterness of exclusion and made them sensitive to the pain of others. And again and again they had found that their God was a God who had a special care for strangers, the despised, the poor and the oppressed. At a time when Christians are a minority of 'cognitive deviants' in western society, we should perhaps be able to learn compassion (suffering or feeling 'together') with other marginalised groups, and recognise that marginalisation offers us special opportunities and challenges.

In the parable of the Good Samaritan (Luke 10:25–37), it is the stranger, the despised and hated foreigner, the heretic excluded from the covenant people, the feared Samaritan who shows himself through his actions to be the neighbour of the Jew, lying wounded and forlorn by the roadside. The stranger acts graciously as a neighbour to the needy person by the roadside. The alien becomes the neighbour. This strange assertion that the alien and the enemy are neighbours, that strangers are neighbours, that people quite different from us are our neighbours, that people we do not know are our neighbours, vastly expands the sphere of moral responsibility. These neighbours are fellow citizens with the saints and with us. And in the earthly city they are entitled to have their dignity protected and their needs recognised. They too are entitled to justice, and given to us to be loved.

Love and Justice

For Christians, love and justice are two sides of the one reality. The liberation theologian, Jose P. Miranda, proclaimed that 'the love that the Bible knows is love-justice', and 'love is not love without a passion for justice'.[6] And the French philosopher Paul Ricoeur is right to say, 'love is co-extensive with justice ... justice is the efficacious, institutional and social realisation of love'.[7] Love is the heart of what justice is about. But we must not suggest that love/justice is a matter only of feeling and emotion. It works not only in face to face relationships, but in structures and social, economic and political processes. And structures of injustice and oppression need to be exposed for what they are and confronted.

The Powers

The New Testament is full of the language of 'principalities and powers'. The 'rulers of this age' do not understand the purposes of God and have 'crucified the King of glory'. But none the less they are 'doomed to pass away' (1 Corinthians 2:6–8). In Christ, God has 'disarmed' the principalities and powers and made a public example of them, triumphing over them (Colossians 2:15). Yet the powers were created by Christ and for him. Subjected to Christ, they find their proper role, function, and limits. Their demonic pretensions are curbed and they become what they were created to be, 'ministering spirits sent forth to serve' (Hebrews 1:14).

Believers as citizens are called to three distinct responses to the powers, in accordance with the context. In the first place, they may struggle against the unruly powers, 'against the world rulers of this present darkness, against the spiritual hosts of wickedness in the heavenly places' (Ephesians 6:12). Second, and in some tension with the first, they are to be in most situations subject to the powers. They should honour and respect them because they have been established by God and have a mandate from him, even if they do not recognise it. Third, the Church is to make known 'the manifold wisdom of God' to the principalities and powers. Because the powers have a significant place in God's design, the Church has a message for, and a responsibility to, the powers.

What do we make of this language in the context of globalisation and our citizenship in earth and heaven? Walter Wink, in three remarkable books, explains the contemporary relevance of the powers.[8] He analyses the powers referred to in the New Testament as determining forces of 'physical psychic and social existence' that have both an inner and an outer aspect.

> Power must become incarnate, institutionalized or systemic in order to be effective. It has a dual aspect, possessing both an outer, visible form (constitutions, judges, police, leaders, office complexes), and an inner, invisible spirit that provides it legitimacy, compliance, credibility and clout.[9]

The World Bank, the International Monetary Fund, the World Trade Organisation and the other institutions of globalisation would seem to deserve the label 'principalities and powers' in our age. We need to learn how to bring them into captivity to Christ, how to make them 'ministering spirits', serving human need and supporting justice and human dignity. They need to be unmasked, exposed and encouraged to fulfil their proper tasks, given them by God.

The Church

The Church, meaning both the world Church, the united and lively Church that is striving to be born, and the congregation of God's people who gather for worship and serve as disciples in the world, includes in its membership many of the poorest and weakest people in the world, and many of the rich and powerful. Within the Church they should be able to challenge and attend to one another, to disturb and challenge one another. This Church should not only speak of God's justice and purposes of good, but manifest and demonstrate in its own life something of the life of the City of God, a kind of appetiser for the good things God has in store for humankind.

Christians as citizens of heaven and resident aliens should be able to point to the Church as a kind of working model of the City of God and its justice and love. Christians should behave as responsible citizens of that city and of the earthly city, taking the lead in caring for one another, and being answerable to one another, and to the needy, unknown stranger who is also a citizen of the City of God.

Perhaps we can point to exemplifications of justice in community in, for example, L'Arche communities, where people with severe learning difficulties live together with others in such a way that the distinction of carer and cared for almost disappears because of the assumption that everyone has something to contribute to the welfare of the community, and the worth and value of each is to be affirmed. Or, perhaps when the Church gathers to celebrate the eucharist, breaking the bread and sharing the cup together, we show just a little of what it is to be the City of God, and the pattern of life that is appropriate for citizens of that city, and the resources that are available to citizens in their relationships and responsibilities. A just society, a just nation, a just globe should display something eucharistic, something lovely in the common life of its citizens, and in its structures and processes.

The Disciplines of Citizenship

Responsible citizens who love their neighbours near and far and have a passion for justice are not simply born, springing forth from their mothers' wombs as fully formed citizens, as it were. They have to be trained, educated, disciplined, so that the selfishness that is so pervasive in a fallen world is curbed, and love with its cognate justice comes to dominate their behaviour and attitudes.

When Jesus was asked what the law was all about he famously replied, '"Love the Lord your God with all your heart, with all your soul, and with all your mind". That is the greatest, the first commandment. The second is like it: "Love your neighbour as yourself." Everything in the law and the prophets hangs on these two commandments.'[10]

Those who asked Jesus the question were Pharisees – the rigorous and relentless enforcers of the law in all its meticulous detail, a law that many good people found oppressive and stultifying – a great network of rules and regulations about all manner of things, many of which seemed absurd, oppressive, out of date and irrelevant. We can disregard those who glibly say that love cannot be commanded. People, especially young people, can be formed, educated, encouraged to love and to do justice with warmth and passion and intelligence. Jesus was, of course, talking about laws, rules, regulations which are intended to enable us to love.

A surprising endorsement of the value of having rules that enable us to love came in the TV programme *Supernanny*, of which I was a devoted viewer. Each week the programme concentrated on one home, one family where the children ran amuck, where amid all the confusion and noise, in the outbursts of temper and anger there was huge uncertainty, and unhappiness.

As the children shouted and refused to eat, or go to bed, or get dressed, it became clear that the children were trying to manipulate the adults, and the adults – sometimes in fact a single mother – were trying desperately to bribe or threaten the children into acceptable behaviour. Again and again one felt that the parents, the carers, and particularly the absent ones who ought to care, were part of the problem. And sometimes they also came from equally disturbed backgrounds. Often they seemed not to have had a chance themselves. They appeared alone, unsupported and often bitter, even against their own children, or the absent spouse or parent. Many of them seemed never to have been loved themselves.

In such a situation rules are non-existent or disregarded. And in the ensuing angry chaos we are reminded that rules are important and necessary.

Into such unhappy situations marches Supernanny. She observes for a week or so what is going on, with mounting alarm, for she knows from experience the devastating implications of not having rules, or having rules to which no one pays attention. She knows the situation is intolerable for the adult or adults involved as parents or as carers. She knows too that it is really hell on earth for the children who are misbehaving. They are craving love, but making it almost impossible to receive love.

Supernanny knows that the wounds and the anger may be passed on from one generation to the next. She knows that if nothing is done, the children will grow up, not into responsible citizens who are concerned about justice and love, but troubled characters who spread their unhappiness around them, the seeds of a harvest of despair. Supernanny knows that in such a situation it is almost impossible for love and happiness to survive and flourish, for good citizens to grow.

The wonder is that out of such a background and experience from time to time a wonderfully loving and caring and gentle mother emerges, determined that her home will be quite different from the family in which she was brought up, and in which she was nearly imprisoned with a life sentence. But usually out of such dysfunctional families without regulations or rules that are observed with some consistency, nothing but trouble emerges. For rules are important and necessary.

There is a wonderful passage in the Letter to the Hebrews about how God educates and disciplines us in order to make us good disciples and good citizens.[11] God disciplines and educates us because he loves us and because he loves humankind. Discipline, that is, is an expression of love. God *bothers* about us. He wants us to grow in love and grace and confidence and hope and gentleness. He wants us, in short, to grow into 'the measure of the stature of the fullness of Christ'.

We all know that our human parents, and we as parents, sometimes lose our tempers, become impatient, treat our children badly, or put our own convenience first. And we all know from the horrific stories in the news that some parents actually abuse their kids. But God loves us and puts our interests first. His discipline is for our good, and to enable us to make our contribution as citizens and neighbours as well as believers. He loves us, and his discipline, upbringing, is to help us, to enable us to love and be loved, to do justice, and care for those who are more needy than we are. When Jesus is asked about the law he replies, quite clearly and emphatically: the heart of all true law is love – love to God and love to our neighbours far and near. Rules and regulations are there to train us in loving, to open us to God's love, and to open our hands to our neighbour's needs. And when laws, rules and regulations do other than this it is time they were reformed or removed.

The Church, Christians believe, is called to be a school of citizenship, both the citizenship of our earthly cities, and our citizenship in heaven, a fellowship where people find new and imaginative ways of loving and doing justice, where we are challenged to respond with generosity to the needs of the world, and nurture faith and hope and love and gentleness even in times of terror and of fear. And Christians should endorse and support all efforts at inculcating the virtues of citizenship, mindful of the teaching of the remarkable story of the judgement of the nations in Matthew 25:31–46. Here, it is not the religious people who are publicly committed to the service of the Lord who receive the blessing; it is rather those who help the needy neighbour because they respond quite spontaneously and lovingly to human need who are blessed and inherit the kingdom:

> For I was hungry and you gave me food, I was thirsty and you gave me something to drink, I was a stranger and you welcomed me, I was naked and you gave me clothing, I was sick and you took care of me, I was a stranger and you welcomed me.[12]

And notice the fact that is often obscured by the translations: in this story it is the 'nations', civil societies, polities, economies, cities, corporations rather than simply individuals who are called to give an account to God of their doings. These bodies act on behalf of many and are called to act justly and lovingly as well as prudently.

Citizens on whose behalf they act should constantly remind them that their mandate is to do justice, and act lovingly and walk humbly.

Notes

1. Pope John Paul II, *Evangelium Vitae,* 20.
2. On this, see Alasdair MacIntyre, *Dependent Rational Animals: Why Human Beings Need the Virtues* (London: Duckworth, 1999).
3. See Duncan B. Forrester, *Christianity and the Future of Welfare* (London: Epworth, 1985).
4. T. H. Marshall, *The Right to Welfare and other Essays* (London: Heinemann, 1981).
5. John Donne, Devotions XVII, in Gordon Mursell, *English Spirituality: from earliest times to 1750* (Louisville: Westminster John Knox Press, 2001), p. 414.
6. J. Miranda, *Marx and the Bible* (London: SCM Press, 1974), p. 62.
7. Cited in J. Miguez Bonino, *Toward a Christian Political Ethics* (London: SCM Press, 1983), p. 114.
8. Walter Wink, *Naming the Powers* (Philadelphia: Fortress, 1984); *Unmasking the Powers* (Philadelphia: Fortress, 1986); *Engaging the Powers* (Minneapolis: Fortress, 1992).
9. Wink, *Unmasking the Powers*, p.4.
10. Matthew 22:37–40 and parallels.
11. Hebrews 12:5–13. The key term in this passage is *paideia* and its cognates. This means education, discipline, acculturation. By a strange irony the *Good News Bible* translates all the *paideia* words in this passage as being concerned with punishment and correction!
12. Matthew 25:35–6

Children's Rights to Citizenship

Kathleen Marshall

What is a Citizen?

As a lawyer, my instinct is to start this paper with a search for a definition. If I am to write about children's rights to citizenship, then I must set out what I mean by that term. This could, however, be a fruitless exercise. A quick online search of the words 'citizen' and 'citizenship' makes it clear that it has no one, simple meaning. There are different gateways to citizenship, and a variety of possible implications of having made one's way across that threshold. The gateway might be birth or descent within a particular community, or a formal grant of citizenship. The implications might include membership of a legal or political community, including the right to vote, the right to be afforded protection by its institutions, and the duty of allegiance to its laws and interests.[1]

Ancient Athens is generally credited as the seed ground for modern ideas of citizenship. The philosopher Aristotle defined a citizen as:

> He who has the power to take part in the deliberative or judicial administration of any state.[2]

Are Children Citizens?

Aristotle described children as 'citizens only in a qualified sense'. They were too young to take part in state administration and therefore 'imperfectly participate in citizenship'.[3] Nevertheless, even at this early date, children were not totally excluded. Aristotle acknowledges their capacity to enter the gateway, while granting them less freedom than adult members to take part in the activities proper to their status. And indeed, in our society, children do not have the right to vote, but they do have a right to be protected by our society's institutions and a duty of allegiance to its laws. If children do not obey the law, there can be consequences. Traditionally, the age of criminal responsibility was linked to the age of reason. Many societies, including our own, followed Aristotle in setting that age at seven. Children below that age were regarded as incapable of committing crimes.[4] Legal responsibility was linked to the possibility of moral agency. Seven was the age of criminal responsibility in Scotland until 1932 when it was generously increased to eight.[5] So if we were, very crudely, to give a citizenship score based on the three criteria of right to vote, protection by state institutions, and duty of allegiance to laws, infants under seven years of age would score one out of three, children aged seven up would score two and adults aged 18 and over would score three. On that model, children would start off as seedling citizens with the right to be protected and would grow into their citizenship by developing the capacity both to break and make the law.

In our society today, there are a number of groups whose capacity has limitations. The mentally ill, the unconscious and those with severe learning difficulties are in a similar position in respect that they may qualify to cross the threshold of citizenship, while at the same time being judged unable to exercise all of the rights and duties, or claim the privileges, of their status. They are unalike in respect that the capacity of children is often defined with regard to chronological age rather than actual capacity, which would be the measure for other groups.

On this analysis, children are indeed citizens, although their capacity to operate as such will have to grow. 'Growing citizens' would not then be about growing into a citizenship conferred or acknowledged at a later date, but about helping young citizens to grow in their ability to act as citizens.[6]

A Wider Perspective: the UN Convention on the Rights of the Child

Citizenship is a formal, adult construct, rooted in a particular form of social organisation – the democratic state. Such a state would have set up institutions to regulate its internal and external relationships and to secure justice and order. A citizen is one who has a voice in shaping the state and its institutions, as well as the right to benefit from the protection afforded by them.[7] At heart, citizenship is about the ability to influence the forces bearing upon you and shaping your life.

In recent years, this same rationale has been the catalyst for an approach to children's rights that complements their status as citizens. In 1989, the General Assembly of the United Nations passed the Convention on the Rights of the Child. This has become the fastest and most widely ratified convention in the history of international law. Only two states have not yet ratified it: Somalia, which has had no recognised government to do so; and the USA, which has its own reasons.

The Convention defines a child as anyone under the age of 18, unless the age of majority is lower. It therefore seeks to protect those whose rights may be 'qualified' as a consequence of their status as minors. Article 12 of the Convention assures children the right to express their views on all matters affecting them, and to have those views taken into account in accordance with age and maturity. In the process of monitoring implementation of the Convention, the UN Committee on the Rights of the Child has made it clear that this right of participation applies not only to decisions which affect the child's individual welfare, it applies also to wider matters affecting children, such as the running of their schools, or community and state affairs. The committee has been keen to ascertain what steps states are taking to implement this aspect of the Convention.

In this respect, it could be said that the Convention gives to children a status more nearly approaching full citizenship than the qualified status accorded by the ancient Greek state. It acknowledges their right to 'take part in the deliberative or judicial administration' of the state, but not necessarily through the same means as adults. It acknowledges the developmental character of childhood, but insists that this should not be a barrier to their participation. It means only that their mode of participation should reflect their abilities, and that the weight given to their views (and weight *must* be given to their views) should be consistent with their level of understanding. The words actually used are 'age and maturity'. It may be helpful at this point to analyse the text in more detail.

Article 12 requires states to:

> assure to the child who is capable of forming his or her own views the right to express those views freely in all matters affecting the child, the views of the child being given due weight in accordance with the age and maturity of the child.

The capacity test is very low, comprising merely the ability to *form* a view. There is no qualification about how considered or informed that view must be. If a child has the ability to form a view, then decision-makers have a responsibility to take whatever steps are necessary to ascertain any view that the child wishes to express, regardless of the child's age, language or particular communication needs.

The weight to be given to that view is to be assessed with reference to both chronological age (an objective criterion about which no guidance is given) and 'maturity' (a subjective judgement with no identified judge). In spite of this vagueness, Article 12 has been the catalyst for much activity at the levels of law, policy and practice, designed to elicit the views of children and young people and feed them into decision-making processes.

Article 3 of the Convention has a different focus. It states that any decisions concerning children (whether as individuals or as groups) should take their *interests* into account as *at least* a primary consideration. This means that, even where children are unable to express their views, whether due to lack of capacity or lack of opportunity, or where they have expressed them but the weight given to them is adversely affected by an assessment of the child's maturity in relation to the matter in question, decision-makers must nevertheless explicitly consider the impact of a proposed decision on affected children and give children's interests appropriate weight. If this were universally respected, it would revolutionise decision-making and greatly enhance the visible participation of children and their status as citizens; for, even when they could not speak, adherence to the Convention would force decision-makers to make space for an assessment of their interests. The Convention would act as an interlocutor for children where they were unable to intervene themselves or carry weight in the decision-making process.

Experiments in Participation

Since the Convention came into effect in the UK in January 1992, there have been many and varied attempts to put it into practice. Some approaches to child and youth participation mimic adult models. They have elected assemblies, formal structures, manifestos and policy papers. In Scotland, the Scottish Youth Parliament, established in 1999, is an elected assembly of around 150 young people aged between 14 and 25 that aims to be a collective national youth voice for all young people in Scotland.[8] At a local level, Young Scot and Dialogue Youth projects in each local authority area aim to help young people aged 12 to 18 to access information and influence the public services provided for them. Young people are involved in the planning and management of Dialogue Youth locally; they are not elected, but link with local youth forums, pupil councils and local members of the Scottish Youth Parliament.[9] The younger age group is catered for by the Children's Parliament, a charity aiming to promote children's active citizenship in Scotland. It is committed to providing sustainable and meaningful opportunities for children aged 9 to 14 to engage in local, national and international democratic processes.[10]

Of course, initiatives such as this do not become established as fully-fledged and operative agencies. They have to grow and learn, and they have to be properly funded if they are to be able to make their mark. They cater for overlapping age groups (which may be an advantage in allowing a choice consistent with the spectrum of developmental needs of children and young people of the same age), and they do not cater for the very youngest group, who also have a right to be heard. Even here, however, some progress is being made towards development of models of participation.[11] Indeed, much good work is being done by preschool establishments across the country that should help shape a more comprehensive approach.

My own role as Commissioner for Children and Young People is yet another development that seeks to give shape and weight to the citizenship of children. Established by the Commissioner for Children and Young People (Scotland) Act 2003, my job is to promote and safeguard the rights of children and young people in Scotland through awareness-raising, monitoring of law, policy and practice, setting standards for good practice, and intervening through formal investigation where the rights of groups of children or young people (not individuals) are potentially infringed.[12] A central part of my role involves listening to children and young people and giving weight to their views, as required by Article 12, and encouraging others to do so. In May 2006, I launched a two-year action plan based upon consultations with children and young people, who were invited to help set my priorities. Almost 16,000 took up the offer.

'The Usual Suspects'?

Sometimes, initiatives designed to respect the rights of children and young people to participate in the democratic project are criticised as being unrepresentative of the general constituency of young people. One is asked whether these assemblies are truly diverse and accessible to children and young people of different backgrounds and abilities, or whether they are populated by 'the usual suspects', those young people who are articulate and educated and attracted by that kind of visible and vocal participation. But this kind of criticism is equally applicable to adult assemblies, at local, national or international level. For so long as the model of power-sharing that citizenship presents is shaped from the top down – by those who already hold power – it will be attractive to those of a similar temperament and disposition.

The potential for cliquishness and exclusivity that this model risks is arguably better acknowledged in the field of child and youth participation than in the adult world. The Scottish Youth Parliament website demonstrates its commitment to an inclusive membership, and the Children's Parliament states that it:

> challenges the notion that only the most confident and articulate can understand or participate in our society. It enables children from all backgrounds and of all abilities to work together to share experiences that make active citizenship a reality.

The Children's Parliament employs a range of interactive and artistic methods to engage with the members of its locally based groups on matters of interest to them. It lays no claim to being a representative model like an adult Parliament, but claims instead:

> We have developed a thematic and holistic approach which underpins our active citizenship programme. Our work is based on children having fun and engaging in projects and investigations in and across our themes which reflect the United Nations Convention on the Rights of the Child.

I sometimes reflect that adult participation might also be more attractive and effective if based on a similar approach!

The Act establishing my office of Commissioner also commits me to paying particular attention to those groups of children and young people who do not have other adequate means to make their views heard. In pursuit of this end I have established contact with numerous disability groups as well as with detached youth workers who work with children and young people on the streets where they 'hang out'. In its early years, my office too is exploring and evaluating different models of participation through formal consultation and standing groups as well as through involvement of young people in matters that are particular to them.[13]

In summary, those models of child and youth participation that mimic adult models to a greater or lesser degree do risk attracting only the 'usual suspects'; but they tend to be more aware than adult groups of the danger of doing so and to take steps to address it. There is also a number of more creative and interactive models of participation being developed for children and young people that might have some relevance also for adults.

Families and Schools

The more relevant the field of decision-making is to a person, the greater the need for participation and 'citizenship'. For children, family and school are critical contexts affecting their quality of life.

Families

1994 was declared by the United Nations as the International Year of the Family, with the motto, 'Building the smallest democracy at the heart of society'. It was proclaimed by the General Assembly of the United Nations only nineteen days after it had passed the Convention on the Rights of the Child. The principles underlying the proclamation echo the preamble to the Convention that

> the family, as the fundamental group of society and the natural environment for the growth and well-being of all its members and particularly children, should be afforded the necessary protection and assistance so that it can fully assume its responsibilities within the community.[14]

Some might balk at the idea of the family as a democracy, pointing in particular to religious exhortations about the obedience of children.[15] But the Convention upholds the authority of parents to provide direction and guidance to their children in a manner consistent with the child's evolving capacities (Article 5). A nuanced understanding of obedience can reconcile authority and participation in the manner of a participative democracy. Indeed, etymologically, effective listening is linked to obedience.

The Latin word *obedire* comes from *ob-audire*, to listen. The beginning of true obedience is when we let someone under our authority speak and we listen to them.[16]

Schools

Debates about education tend to be bedevilled by conflicting notions about whether pupils are participants in their education or products of it. Sometimes the debate uses the language of consumerism, which raises the question about who the consumers are: the parents or the pupils? In the 1980s, the development of School Boards in Scotland acknowledged the legitimate claims of parents to have a role in the running of the school.[17] Pupils had no right of involvement, although senior pupils, aged over 16, could be co-opted. The Scottish Schools (Parental Involvement) Act 2006 abolished School Boards and replaced them with Parent Forums and Parent Councils. A school's strategy for parental involvement must take account of the views of pupils, and Parent Councils must also communicate with pupils.

This history evidences a developing acknowledgement of the interest of pupils in shaping the environment and activities that form a large part of their lives. A more explicit focus on the rights of pupils, consistent with the Convention on the Rights of the Child, is evident in an Act of the year 2000, which requires that

> the school development plan should include an account of the ways in which, and extent to which, the headteacher of the school will – (a) consult the pupils in attendance at the school; and (b) seek to involve them, when decisions require to be made concerning the everyday running of the school.[18]

Welcome as this is, it still falls short of a legal requirement to set up a mechanism for involving pupils that satisfies prescribed quality standards.

But, if there were quality standards, what should they be? School pupil councils may look great on paper, but may not make the pupils feel included. A 2005 survey of young people in Scotland showed that younger pupils were more positive about their school councils than teenagers were. Of the respondents, 30 per cent said their school council worked well, but only 14 per cent thought it had made a difference to their lives.[19]

Effective pupil councils may be part of the answer, but they are not all of it. Citizenship education is a hot topic today, with initiatives across the UK. Scotland has taken a different approach from the other nations based on learning by doing. Learning and Teaching Scotland explains:

> The Scottish approach to education for citizenship differs from others areas of the United Kingdom, because it has not introduced a new subject or curricular area called 'Citizenship'. Instead, it is expected that all subjects will make their relevance to education for citizenship explicit, and that the purposes and issues associated with citizenship will be developed through whole-school and cross curricular activities.

Recommended learning and teaching approaches include:

- participation by young people in decision-making, within classroom activities and at whole-school levels
- development of authentic community links
- active approaches to learning, including discussion, debate and investigation, and
- whole-school activities that raise awareness of citizenship issues, ethical decision-making and shared values.[20]

The development of 'citizenship education' is designed to help children and young people to grow in their citizenship.

The model recommended by Learning and Teaching Scotland links citizenship activities within the school with the child's most immediate social environment – with what is happening in the rest of the community. It is a potentially valuable but high-risk strategy. If schools that present this model fail to engage their pupils or to respond adequately to their concerns, they risk disillusioning children and young people even more.

A Citizenship Ceremony?

In March 2008, Lord Goldsmith fulfilled his commission to write a report on citizenship for the Prime Minister.[21] Among other things, he suggested citizenship ceremonies for young people who had completed their citizenship education at school. These would be modelled on the ceremonies for new citizens introduced in 2002 and might include an oath of allegiance to the Queen. Although only a small part of a much larger report, this proposal attracted much media attention and public comment, most of it adverse. One of the objections was that this seemed to imply that young people were not already citizens, a perception strengthened by Lord Goldsmith's reported statement that such ceremonies would be 'a way of marking that passage of being a student of citizenship to a citizen in practice'.[22] Others derided it as an empty symbol and emphasised the need to make citizenship a real and significant concept for young people by ensuring that their active participation is real and effective.[23]

Conclusion

Children clearly have rights at every age and responsibilities from a very early age. If we are to support their growth as citizens and moral agents, we should actively empower them to shape the world around them and learn to exercise that agency. But it need not be all or nothing. The Convention on the Rights of the Child acknowledges the developmental nature of childhood. It does not require that children be given the power of adults. Neither does it expect that they be attributed the full responsibility for their actions in the same way as adults. Power and responsibility grow together towards mature moral agency and the full flowering of citizenship.

Notes

1. In March 2008, Lord Goldsmith presented the Prime Minster with a report on citizenship that he had been commissioned to undertake. In 'Citizenship: Our Common Bond', Lord Goldsmith identifies three categories of legal rights and responsibilities inherent in citizenship: right of abode and free movement; right of protection and duty of allegiance; civic rights (including the right to vote); and social and economic rights. He observed that there are six different categories of citizenship embracing different aspects of these rights and responsibilities. The report also asserts that, 'a core element of the shared bond of citizenship is to participate in society' (p. 89).
2. Aristotle, *Politics*, III.1; 11.
3. Aristotle, *Politics*, III.1; 5.
4. Note that the Code of Canon Law of the Roman Catholic Church still identifies seven as the age of reason (Canon 97). Below that age an infant is considered not responsible for himself.
5. Children and Young Persons (Scotland) Act 1932, section 14. See the discussion on the Scottish Law Commission Report on Age of Criminal Responsibility (No. 185) (Edinburgh: The Stationery Office, 2002), para. 2.5.
6. This begs a question about whether the rules about the most visible manifestation of citizenship – the right to vote – should be assessed on the basis of actual capacity rather than, as now, a blanket criterion of age. Many other aspects of the lives of children are now regulated by assessment of capacity rather than chronological age; a development encouraged by the 1989 United Nations Convention on the Rights of

the Child. Should voting too hinge upon individual assessment, or would that be too cumbersome? In other areas of children's lives, a workable balance has been sought through the introduction of a 'presumption' of capacity at a certain age. This might be fixed and irrebuttable (such as the presumption that a child under eight years of age has no criminal responsibility) or rebuttable (such as the presumption in family law that a child aged 12 or over has sufficient age and maturity to form a view in relation to decisions about his or her upbringing). But what kind of capacity would we be assessing?: the capacity to understand, differentiate between and judge candidates from different political parties?; the ability to understand their manifestos?; the ability to understand their communal responsibilities in a democratic society as well as their individual wants and needs? By those standards, how many adults would pass the test?

7. Although, as the ancient Romans discovered, when a society expands its interests through the acquisition of empire, it has to extend some basic rights also to non-citizens. Thus the 'ius civile' that applied to Roman citizens had to be supplemented by the 'ius gentium' – the law of the nations. See J. Muirhead, *Historical Introduction to the Private Law of Rome* (2nd edn, revised and edited by H. Goudy; London: A. & C. Black, 1899), pp. 225ff.
8. See www.scottishyouthparliament.org.uk.
9. See www.dialogueyouth.org.
10. See www.childrensparliament.org.uk.
11. For examples, see the Participation Portal on the website of Scotland's Commissioner for Children and Young People: www.sccyp.org.uk.
12. See www.sccyp.org.uk.
13. See, for example, the involvement of disabled young people in *Handle With Care: the Moving and Handling of Children and Young People with Disabilities*; and of young people who are or have been in public care, in *Sweet 16? The Age of Leaving Care in Scotland*. Both reports were published in 2008 and are available at www.sccyp.org.uk.
14. The principles underlying the Declaration were downloaded from http://www.un.org/esa/socdev/family/IntObs/IYF/princ.html (accessed 7 March 2008).
15. The religious requirements of obedience are explored in K. Marshall and P. Parvis, *Honouring Children: the human*

rights of the child in Christian perspective (Edinburgh: Saint Andrew Press, 2004), Ch. 7.2.2.1.
16. T. Radcliffe, *Sing A New Song* (Dublin: Dominican Publications, 1999), p. 35.
17. School Boards (Scotland) Act 1988. See www.schoolboard-scotland.com.
18. Standards in Scotland's Schools etc. Act 2000, Section 6(3).
19. Questions on school councils commissioned by SCCYP as part of the *Being Young in Scotland* survey commissioned by Youthlink Scotland in 2005.
20. See www.ltscotland.org.uk.
21. Goldsmith, 'Citizenship: Our Common Bond', supra.
22. Lord Goldsmith, quoted in 'Pupils "to take allegiance oath"'. BBC News website (11 March 2008).
23. The BBC News (supra) also reported the comment of Labour peer Baroness Kennedy, 'I think this is a serious mistake – I think it's puerile and I think it's rather silly'.

Education for Citizenship in Scottish Schools

Pamela Munn

Introduction

In the recent past there has been a worldwide resurgence of interest in education for citizenship from politicians and educators (Biesta and Lawly 2006; Osler and Starkey 2005).[1] In England and Wales, citizenship was one of the five cross-curricular themes introduced in 1990, supplementing the 1988 Education Act, which introduced the national curriculum (Faulks 2006).[2] However, it was not until the election of a Labour Government in 1997 that a more comprehensive attempt to define education for citizenship was made through a review group set up by the then Secretary of State for Education, David Blunkett. The review group's report (Crick 1998)[3] was followed by a citizenship order making education for citizenship a compulsory foundation subject at secondary level (for pupils 11–16) in the national curriculum in England and Wales, with 5 per cent of the timetable being devoted to it. Primary schools are also required to show, through inspection, how they are preparing their pupils for citizenship. At the same time, the Labour Government held a referendum in Scotland about the desirability of establishing a devolved administration with its own parliament. The overwhelming vote in favour and the holding of the first Scottish parliamentary elections in 1999 were key features of the context in which education for citizenship emerged as a priority for development in education policy. This has taken a rather different form from that in England and Wales.

The establishment of a devolved parliament in Scotland brought much more direct political control over education (and other aspects of domestic policy), albeit within a British state which retained control of economic, foreign and defence policy. For the purposes of this chapter, it is important to note that Scotland does not have a statutory national curriculum, preferring to rely on national guidelines and on syllabuses underpinning national qualifications taken by the majority of young people around 16, 17 or 18 years of age, to drive what is taught in schools. This means that curriculum innovation largely depends on consensus underpinned by a national examinations system, a national inspection system and local authority monitoring and review. There is a national curriculum agency, Learning and Teaching Scotland (LTS), whose role is to advise the Scottish government on curriculum matters and to provide curriculum support and advice to schools.

Scotland and Scottish education are not, of course, immune to global concerns affecting advanced industrial economies. These might be summed up as the importance of school systems to improving economic performance through the production of a skilled and adaptable workforce. The focus on the measurement of national standards of academic attainment and on international comparisons of attainment with those of our key economic competitors is a manifestation of this global concern. In addition, the social and moral development of young people is seen as key. This interest might be seen partly as a response to a rise in youth crime and the moral panic that accompanies reporting of incidents of indiscipline in schools across the globe. It might also be seen as a response to the increasingly diverse nature of nation states in terms of populations, religions and values and the increasingly explicit role assigned to schools in promoting social cohesion. Other influences include concern in democracies about declining voter turn-out in national and local elections and the growing prominence of rights-based approaches to achieving human security and development. To coin Ozga's (2005) usage,[4] while there are global forces at work, there is a need to recognise that education policy is both 'travelling' and 'embedded'. Gunther (2006:115) summarises as follows:

> while regulating educational purposes to deliver an economically productive workforce is travelling to and around the UK, it is also the case that local practice, culture and requirements are embedded, and hence mediate and possibly act as a barrier to how travelling policy is read.[5]

Analysis of the development and implementation of education for citizenship in Scottish schools can thus tell us something about the assumptions underpinning the approach to curriculum development and assumptions about the purposes of education for citizenship. This is considered at the end of the chapter.

Education for Citizenship in Scottish Schools

A national review group was set up in 1999 by the then Scottish Consultative Council on the Curriculum (predecessor to LTS) to review arrangements for education for citizenship 3–18 and to set out a curriculum framework for further development. It was the first major consultation document to emerge from this body in a devolved Scotland. The review group grew out of previous work by the Consultative Council on the distinctively Scottish nature of the curriculum. It was also partly a response to developments in England and Wales and, partly too, a recognition that education policy was likely to be a major priority of the soon to be established Scottish Parliament and Executive. The final report, *Education for Citizenship in Scotland: a paper for discussion and development* (Learning and Teaching Scotland 2002)[6] set out the key purposes of education for citizenship and the ways in which these might be pursued in schools.[7] The report was the subject of widespread consultation and was endorsed by the then Education Minister, Cathy Jamieson. It was seen as congruent with the national priorities in education which had been established by the first Education Act passed by the new Scottish Parliament in 2000 and has subsequently featured heavily in the major curriculum review and development programme known as *A Curriculum for Excellence*. Indeed, one of the key purposes of the school curriculum put forward by that programme is the production of responsible citizens. The report had a number of important features, summarised as follows:

- Education for citizenship was seen as a key overarching purpose of the curriculum. It was not seen as a separate subject requiring a specific space in the school timetable.
- The purpose of education for citizenship was to develop young people's capability for thoughtful and responsible participation in political, economic, social and cultural life.
- Children and young people were seen as citizens now rather than citizens in waiting.
- It emphasised that young people learn most about citizenship by being active citizens and urged schools to model the kind of society in which active citizenship is encouraged. In particular, it encouraged schools to promote young people's active participation in decision-making and to develop a participatory ethos.
- It encouraged schools to develop the capabilities outlined above in ways that motivated young people

to be active and responsible members of their communities, drawing attention to the local, national and global and thus to multiple identities in the modern world.

- It recognised that schools were one influence among many on young people's ideas about citizenship.
- It set out knowledge and understanding, skills and competences, values and dispositions and the creative and enterprising attitudes which schools could promote through learning experiences.
- It set out an agenda for development, recognising that schools were already doing good work in many areas.
- It drew attention to values conflicts, power relationships, and the importance of developing critical autonomy in young people.
- It recognised that the paper was not the last word on the subject and that there was a need to share experience and ideas as schools discussed and experimented with the suggestions in the paper.[8]

LTS developed a supporting website (www.ltscotland.com/citizenship) which provided case studies of school developments, audit materials for schools to use to help to evaluate their existing provision and to plan coherence and progression in their education for citizenship programmes, as well as lists of resources to support learning and teaching. A number of well-attended conferences promoting education for citizenship were also held in different parts of the country to raise awareness and share experiences among schools.

Accountability and reporting mechanisms of course are very influential on what schools do. The focus on development and experimentation was echoed in the performance indicators for education for citizenship which were developed as part of national priority 4, values and citizenship. This national priority asks schools to: 'work with parents to teach pupils respect for self and one another and their interdependence with other members of their neighbourhood and teach them the duties and responsibilities of citizenship in a democratic society'. Schools and local authorities were asked to report on their progress in achieving this priority for the first time in 2005. The performance measure is narrative, in that schools are invited to report on the range and scale of activities offered to pupils which encourage and support the development of education for citizenship. In the supporting documents for school reports, areas such as curriculum strategy, range and authenticity of learning experience and participatory ethos are suggested as areas on which schools may wish to report (www.nationalpriorities.org.uk). In addition, schools are directed to a variety of sources from which they can learn more about the characteristics of schools, classrooms and teachers that foster citizenship.

Her Majesty's Inspectorate of Education has likewise adopted a permissive approach to evaluating the effectiveness of education for citizenship in Scottish schools.[9] Its guide to schools on self-evaluating provision for education for citizenship contains eight quality indicators to help schools assess the range and quality of their contribution. These are:

- the extent to which citizenship is included in the curriculum overall … and how well different courses and programmes relate to one another;
- the quality of young people's learning and personal and social development and growth;
- the quality of the school's links with other groups and organisations and the extent to which these … support and develop aspects of citizenship;

- the extent to which the quality of the climate and relationships support the development of citizenship;
- how effective education for citizenship is in promoting and developing an ethos of equality and fairness within the school;
- how effectively (schools) involve parents and the wider community in education for citizenship.[10]

The publication goes on to offer advice about evaluating school provision against these indicators and provides examples of very good provision. It also draws attention to other relevant HMIe publications including those on international education.

Thus, the background against which schools were encouraged by their local authorities or national organisations to provide case studies of education for citizenship was enabling and permissive. There was no numeric performance indicator against which schools were to be judged, such as the number of pupil councils in operation or the number of young people engaged in voluntary activities. Rather there was a fairly clear message that schools should develop provision in a way that seemed appropriate to them, albeit against a general framework of the aims and purposes of education for citizenship. Furthermore there were no league tables of school effectiveness in education for citizenship.

Experiences in Schools

This section relies largely on information derived from schools' own accounts of their work to develop education for citizenship published either on the LTS website or via case studies published by the Scottish Schools Ethos Network. (See Ross et al. 2007[11] for a description of the sample of work researched and the approach adopted to analysing the content of these case studies.) It is worth remembering, however, that the number of case studies available is small, around sixteen each for primary and secondary schools with an additional three reports of good practice on the LTS website. The Scottish Schools Ethos Network published around forty case studies on a participatory ethos – a key feature of education for citizenship in general and a preliminary analysis of eight of these was undertaken. The other major source of information is from HMIe, gathered through their routine general inspections of schools and in their more focused 'Portraits' series which aims to provide an overview of particular areas of the curriculum and relate the findings to *A Curriculum for Excellence*. In its landmark report *Improving Scottish Education*,[12] published in 2006 and providing an overview of the system as a whole, HMIe summed up its view of the state of progress in education for citizenship in Section 3.1.

> Schools also have increased their emphasis on citizenship. Many are giving some more attention to involving young people in decision-making. Some have used curriculum inserts to explore issues such as citizenship and the law or anti-racism. However, practice is uneven within and across schools. The development of pupils' understanding of values and citizenship, including the ability to hold informed views and make judgements, depends on the acquisition of knowledge and critical thinking skills. Systematic curriculum planning to ensure that pupils are well prepared for political, social, economic and cultural involvement in society and to participate in significant decisions at school is not yet common.
>
> As schools develop citizenship further, they need to ensure that values associated with responsible citizenship are also promoted through pupils' everyday classroom experiences and the life of the school as a community.

A published review of developments in schools from HMIe in 2006 provides a more detailed overview of the strengths and areas for improvement in school practice. There are also seven items on citizenship in the 'Journey to Excellence' series from HMIe,[13] which is available as a curriculum development resource to schools.

There has, however, been no major research in Scotland on the implementation of education for citizenship across the country in contrast to the major longitudinal work being undertaken in England by the National Foundation for Educational Research. (See www.nfer.ac.uk for further details on the Citizenship Education Longitudinal Study.) What can be concluded from the evidential base currently available?

- Most schools have established mechanisms to enable pupils or their representatives to participate in decision-making about aspects of school life. The most common of these was a school council. We know little from the cases studies about how elections to the council take place, how agenda items are decided upon and how decisions are made and conveyed to the school as a whole. Where such information is available, a great deal of thought has been given to these matters. For example, one account revealed that the school council had a budget of £2,000 per annum, designed to signal that it was a serious committee with the power to do things.
- Much of the focus of the early work of school councils has been on the school environment, with improvements in the playground or in the toilets being most common.
- There has been some pupil decision-making about the curriculum especially in the area of personal and social education.
- Reports of other forms of pupil participation abound and include classroom as well as school-level matters, for example on behaviour, peer counselling, and buddy

schemes whereby an older child befriends a younger one and 'looks out' for them. Most often these kinds of schemes relate to ways of tackling bullying. We found it interesting that the focus was on ways of tackling anti-social behaviour rather than a deeper consideration of the nature of schooling in which such behaviour took place.

- In general, participation mechanisms for pupils conveyed the impression of pupils being incorporated into the organisational structure of the schools to improve ways of doing things rather than to challenge the existing systems. The mechanisms seem to be being used to enable the schools to do what they always do, but more efficiently and effectively. The paired reading, buddy and peer counselling schemes, for example, all intrinsically worthwhile, might be seen as helping to develop capability for thoughtful and responsible participation in social life, helping others, particularly those in difficulty of one kind or another. It was not clear whether they also involved discussion and debate about why such schemes were needed in schools at all. If such discussion did take place it would be interesting to know how much explanations lay in the individual agency of pupils and how much lay in considerations of the structures and functions of schooling.
- The development of political literacy – an understanding of the way our system of government functions and its strengths and weaknesses – did not feature strongly in the case studies. There are examples of pupils being involved in mock elections and of pursuing particular issues affecting their school experience to local and parliamentary levels. There are also reports of pupil involvement in charitable activities, environmental projects and the like. These are all intrinsically worthwhile but the economic, social and political dimensions of these can be underdeveloped.

- Examples of planned curriculum progression so that young people have the opportunity to build up a fuller understanding of contemporary local, national and global issues are scarce. There are some examples of Fair Trade featuring as a curriculum topic and of school debates on controversial issues but it is difficult to build up a comprehensive picture of curriculum provision, largely because of the embedded nature of education for citizenship across the curriculum. The developments associated with *A Curriculum for Excellence* may spur on school curriculum planning and the development of interdisciplinary work. This latter is more difficult to plan and manage in large secondary schools where the curriculum is more clearly organised in terms of individual subject disciplines than in primary schools.
- Progression in terms of pupil participation can also be lacking especially when pupils move from primary to secondary schools. They can leave primaries having exercised considerable responsibility as school or class representatives, or been actively involved in buddy schemes, only to find that they are treated as novices on entry to secondary school.
- The outcomes of involving pupils more actively in decision-making are almost always positively reported and key among them were improvements in behaviour. This was seen as the result of developing a sense of collective and individual responsibility for behaviour. The following extracts give a flavour of these.
    - Happier, quieter lunchtimes (Case Study 24).
    - [We] have not excluded any pupils for two years (Case Study 21).
    - I was able to form positive relationships throughout the school (Teacher Case Study 41).

- Another key theme was improvement in learning a range of skills such as listening, communication, problem solving, working in a team via curriculum projects, and exercising choice.

Conclusions

Three main points emerge from this account which have a bearing on curriculum innovation in general as well as education for citizenship in particular.

The first is that any curriculum innovation which attempts to build on the existing practice in schools, rather than portray itself as a radical departure, takes time, even when based on widespread consent. From the publication of the LTS paper and its acceptance by the Minister of Education in 2002, the impression one gets from the evidence available six years later is of the patchiness of developments. In part, this is due to the complexity of an innovation which is embedded across the curriculum rather than a specific subject on the timetable. As the LTS paper suggested, it is all too easy to slide from an appreciation that education for citizenship is everyone's responsibility to being nobody's responsibility, especially in a large and complex organisation which is the secondary school. There is always the tendency for teachers to believe that they are already 'doing citizenship' and that they are the examples of good practice that are being built on and that they need do nothing more.

The position is further complicated by the absence of numeric performance indicators and the injunction to schools to develop in ways that are appropriate to them. The reliance on a narrative approach to performance puts considerable onus on local authority monitoring systems to report developments or lack of them and to take appropriate action. There does not seem to be any incentive for local authorities to do this in any systematic and thorough way. This issue has particular salience in the context of the new 'Concordat'[14] (2007) between local authorities and the Scottish Government which lays clear responsibilities on local authorities to report their performance against key performance indicators across the services they provide. How well placed local authorities are to provide information which is required is a matter of a great deal of interest and speculation.

The second point refers to policy and practice learning across the system. HMIe (2006)[15] has referred to the need for more professional development opportunities to be made available to teachers. We know that one approach is to share experiences of and ideas about education for citizenship among teachers themselves. Such opportunities need to relate to curriculum planning and progression, interdisciplinary working, curriculum mapping and monitoring as well as learning and teaching. Perhaps the *Curriculum for Excellence* learning outcomes and the professional development associated with these will provide one route for local and national development opportunities. A trickier question is the way in which local authorities might learn from each other about strengths and weaknesses in their approach to education for citizenship.

Third, what does education for citizenship tell us about the embedded practices of the Scottish school system? These might be summarised at curriculum policy level as:

- A commitment to take forward curriculum development by consensus. This can lead to a slow pace of development and implementation, justified on the grounds of greater acceptance of reform by all concerned, rather than surface compliance.
- An over-reliance on numeric accountability systems to provide 'health checks' on performance and the corresponding underdevelopment of narrative systems especially at local levels. As we have seen in this

> chapter, it is HMIe who have been publishing accounts of the implementation of education for citizenship and identifying areas for improvement. This has significant implications if we move away from some numeric performance indicators in the future and increasing reliance is placed on local authorities. It is particularly difficult to give a comprehensive account of education for citizenship because it is embedded across the curriculum and deals with hard to measure phenomena such as values, beliefs and attributes. Yet, if we began from a notion of the entitlement of pupils to certain kinds of curriculum experiences, we could map the provision of such experiences and then seek to find ways of evaluating their quality.

In terms of curriculum practice, we have seen the willingness, energy and commitment of many teachers to innovate and use imaginative techniques and opportunities to engage with education for citizenship. For the most part their accounts portray, unsurprisingly, an ingrained developmental approach to children based on their age – seen in primary–secondary transition for example. They also convey a key purpose of pupil participation being a desire to improve the school's way of doing things, for example in developing positive behaviour, or improving induction arrangements for new pupils, or engaging pupils more in learning. This is all very understandable. However, extending the boundaries of pupil participation to include active engagement in what to learn and how to learn still seems some way off and perhaps implies a 'teacher knows best' approach. This is deep and difficult territory, raising the nature of teacher authority, professionalism and accountability. It is a debate we need to have if we are serious that children are citizens now rather than citizens in waiting whose rights and responsibilities, as well as those of teachers and other adults working in schools, need recognition. It recognises that education for citizenship is not just about knowledge and skills but needs to involve a conscious articulation of the cultural environment in which citizenship is exercised, and which future citizens can help to shape and reshape.

Notes

1. G. Biesta and R. Lawly, 'From teaching citizenship to learning democracy: overcoming individualism in research, policy and practice', *Cambridge Journal of Education* 36, 1 (2006), pp. 63–79; A. Osler and H. Starkey, *Education for Democratic Citizenship* (British Educational Research Association, 2005). www.bera.ac.uk/pdfs/OslerStarkey, BERAReview2006.pdf (accessed 14 March 2006).
2. K. Faulks, 'Rethinking citizenship education in England: some lessons from contemporary social and political theory', *Education, Citizenship and Social Justice* 1, 2 (2006), pp. 123–40.
3. Bernard Crick, *Education for Citizenship and the Teaching of Democracy in Schools: Final Report of the Advisory Group on Citizenship* (London: QCA, 1998).
4. J. Ozga, 'Modernising the Education Workforce: a perspective from Scotland', *Educational Review* 57, 2 (2005), pp. 207–19.
5. H. Gunther, 'Teacher leadership: challenges and opportunities', *Scottish Educational Review*, 37 (2006), Special Edition: Teacher Education and Professional Development, pp. 114–23.
6. Learning and Teaching Scotland, *Education for Citizenship in Scotland: a paper for discussion and development* (Dundee and Glasgow: LTS, 2002).
7. Nurseries and other educational establishments were also included. School is used as convenient shorthand.
8. Learning and Teaching Scotland, 2002.
9. HMIe. *How Good is our School? Education for Citizenship* (Edinburgh: HM Inspectorate of Education, 2003).
10. HMIe, 2003, p. 3.
11. H. Ross, P. Munn and J. Brown, 'What counts as student voice in active citizenship case studies? Education for Citizenship in Scotland', *Education, Citizenship and Social Justice* 2, 3 (2007), pp. 237–56.

12. HMIe, *Improving Scottish Education* (Edinburgh: HM Inspectorate of Education, 2006).
13. www.hmie.gov.uk, Journey to Excellence Zone (accessed 12 May 2008).
14. www.scotland.gov.uk/Resource/Doc/923/0054147.pdf (accessed 16 June 2008).
15. HMIe, *A Portrait of Current Practice in Scottish Schools and pre-School Centres: Education for Citizenship* (Edinburgh: HM Inspectorate of Education, 2006).

Two Views of Education for Citizenship

Lindsay Paterson and Ross Bond

This short note concentrates on the question: what is the most appropriate intellectual preparation for citizenship? It describes two views that have prevailed in Scotland over the last century about what a curriculum for citizenship might be. The contrast between the two views raises difficult questions for what we might currently mean by citizenship education.

Skills

We start with the view that is now dominant: the belief that education for citizenship requires that students acquire certain skills and capacities, and that at best they should learn how to engage critically with people in authority.

A particularly influential instance of this view is the response by Learning and Teaching Scotland – the body which is responsible for advising on the school curriculum – to the report of the working party that its predecessor set up to investigate education for citizenship in Scotland; that report was the most thorough and careful recent consideration of this question in Scotland. LTS agreed with its working party that citizenship should pervade the curriculum, and should not be tied to any specific body of knowledge:

> Education for citizenship should aim to develop the capability for thoughtful and responsible participation in political, economic, social and cultural life. This capability is rooted in knowledge and understanding, in a range of generic skills and competencies, including 'core skills', and in a variety of personal qualities and dispositions. It finds expression through creative and enterprising approaches to issues and problems.[1]

This clearly places the greatest emphasis on skills. Even by '*knowledge and understanding*' it turns out that LTS mean skills too: 'appreciating the need to base opinions, views and decisions on relevant knowledge and on a critical evaluation and balanced interpretation of evidence'.[2]

Such a view is widespread, and indeed is merely one instance of a more general belief that the curriculum for whatever topic should mainly be concerned with developing skills rather than imparting knowledge. Another current example relates to the expansion of higher education. More than one half of people in Scotland now enter higher education by age 21, and so some experience of it is becoming as important a route into adulthood as experience of a full course of secondary education was half a century ago. Our investigation of academics' own views of the role of critical citizenship has been funded by the Leverhulme Trust, as part of a wider project on national identity.[3] Full details are in the papers cited in footnote 3; the conclusions, however, may be illustrated by a couple of quotations. In Scotland, we found that academics were inclined to encourage critical thinking. For example, one lecturer in languages said:

> (in my particular field) questioning authorities, knowing the past, being prepared to think across the time periods, respect for different cultures, ... In university generally, I think if universities aren't helping students to learn to question authority, then I don't know what we're doing.

Such views were by no means confined to people working in the humanities or social sciences; for example, the following was said by an engineer:

> If you have people who are going through the university system, if they have a good experience of that system opening their eyes, getting them to think critically about things, then that's the kind of population who can debate things like GM crops or cloning or whatever and can debate it in a rational way, rather than the kind of tabloid way in which these things are dealt with now.

On the whole, academics in Scotland were somewhat more inclined to foster critical citizenship in these ways than academics were in England. The difference should not be exaggerated: there was widespread support for civic interpretations of higher education in each country. In each, most academic teachers encouraged their students to be socially responsible, to put their education to social use. In each country, too, academics were themselves involved in many kinds of engagement with society beyond the university, activities such as contributing to the news media, advising policy makers, providing consultancy for commercial businesses and giving public lectures to wide audiences. Nevertheless, there were differences between Scotland and England in the ways in which a civic role for academic teaching was defined, and in the manner in which these views interacted with academics' own sense of national identity.

In Scotland, the most enthusiastic support for critical citizenship came from academics whose own identity was 'Scottish', not 'British' – the two quotations above come from such people – who made up about 28 per cent of academics in Scotland, or about 48 per cent of those who themselves took their first degree at a Scottish university. Scottish identity has itself been politicised in the last quarter of a century, as a consequence of tensions between the

Scottish and English political majorities in the 1980s and 1990s. The resulting debates raised many questions about the nature of democracy and civic responsibility, and these in turn were influential on the discussions that surrounded the setting up of the Scottish Parliament in 1999. So it is perhaps not surprising that people who adhere to a 'Scottish' identity would interpret their educational role as being partly civic.

People in Scotland who called themselves both 'British' and 'Scottish' were not straightforwardly less civic-minded, but they did not see their pedagogical role as encouraging students to apply their critical capacities to democratic debate as such. Citizenship was something that should be exercised through employment. Moreover, that view was the common one in England, regardless of the academics' own sense of national identity.

In conclusion to this first section, then, we can say that the dominant view of education for citizenship is now that it is about developing a social version of the skills of critical thinking. There is variation as to the domain in which these capacities should be exercised – civic or economic – but not as to their fundamental purposes.

Engaging with a Tradition

Thus, there is little support nowadays for the view that education should pass on the best that has been thought and said (Matthew Arnold's definition of culture). In our survey of academics, such views were expressed only by people on the right politically, and in Scotland only among people who expressed an exclusively British identity. But that belief used to be dominant in Scottish education, as in many other places. It was held that engaging with a cultural tradition was the best preparation for citizenship.

A good example of that in Scotland is the role which the study of literature had in Scottish secondary education in the first four decades of the twentieth century, a period when secondary schooling was emerging as a distinct stage for the first time.[4] It was believed – by teachers, inspectors, policy makers in government, and university professors – that the subject which was called English should be at the heart of a truly secondary education, and that, through English, pupils could learn how to live in society.

The view was that developing this social capacity required engaging with a tradition. For example, one of the early and influential thinkers on this was S. S. Laurie, the first professor of education at Edinburgh University (from 1876 until 1903). He believed that a nation's character could be discovered in 'the literary expression of its way of looking at the world', and that through literature people may enter 'on the inheritance which the past has bequeathed'. The aim of literary studies should be 'the making of a good citizen'.

Likewise, the standard specification for the Leaving Certificate from 1895 until after 1939 required that candidates for Higher Grade English should have 'some acquaintance with the authorship and period of the leading masterpieces of our literature', and should be based on close, critical reading:

> knowledge of literary history should in all cases be based upon a first-hand acquaintance with literature itself, acquired by the careful study of a few well-chosen masterpieces supplemented by more cursory reading in a wider but no less carefully selected range of English classics.

As the Scottish Council for Research in Education said in a report on English in 1931, 'to teach English to pupils of any age is to help them to satisfy ... the need to understand others and to be understood by them'. This echoed Adam Smith's view that we become social beings by learning to judge our own actions through an imaginary 'impartial spectator' expressing society's norms and values, and his belief also that one effective way of stimulating that imagination was through learning about literary characterisation with its capacity to enable us to stand outside ourselves.

In that sense, literature took on a role in the emerging secondary system rather akin to that which common sense philosophy played in the Scottish universities in the nineteenth century. That system of thought held that the purpose of learning is to clarify and purify the common sense of the community. It developed originally as a response to the radical scepticism of David Hume: philosophers such as Thomas Reid believed that to doubt all obligations as anything other than ingrained habits would be to undermine the very basis of social order. His and his successors' response to Hume did have some similarities with the mainstream European response, through Kant to Hegel: both that and the Scottish development sought stable coherence in human thought that could, among other goals, keep society from falling apart as industrialism disrupted all sorts of old social bonds. The Scottish development was less intellectually distinguished and sustained than the European one, but also much more practically grounded: it was as much a pedagogical response as a purely philosophical one, and provided the guiding principles of the education received by students passing through the Scottish universities in the nineteenth century.

It was not a revolutionary philosophy, although it was mildly reformist. It was strengthened in this regard by the influence back upon it of German idealism in the late nineteenth century, attaching the sense of civic duty quite firmly to the state. So this renovated tradition was available to the growing professional class of the twentieth century as a highly ethical and deeply paternalistic account of their role.

They also then sought to extend its influence to the society as a whole, through the reforms to secondary schooling in the first few decades of the century. These schools gradually became the only way of entering professional careers, whether directly or through universities and colleges. The culturally unifying core of their curriculum was literary studies, approached in a civic manner. Unlike in England, literature in these Scottish schools was not what has been described as a 'poor man's Latin': it came to replace Latin even in schools serving mainly middle-class areas. In contrast to Germany and France (and in common with England), it was not an enfeebled substitute for philosophy: the mind and the moral faculty could be trained, it was believed, by rigorous attention to linguistic analysis of texts, and by the discussion of the philosophical issues that were raised by novels, poems, plays and essays.

Although at this time only about one in three pupils entered a secondary course, and only one in twenty did gain the full Leaving Certificate, this role for English carried over into the much more widely accessible secondary system after the Second World War, and survived to shape the character of secondary courses in comprehensive schools at least until the 1980s. In any case, even when only a minority of pupils took a full secondary course, they went on to become the Scottish professional classes of the second half of the twentieth century. In that capacity, they exercised their intensely moral sense of citizenship – acquired through such courses – to shape the society that Scotland became.

Questions

Nevertheless, despite the legacy, we have moved away from this view now. One reason is exemplified in the inadequacy of the term 'masterpieces' in the regulations for Higher English quoted above. How do we define cultural literacy when what we have inherited from the past excluded the contributions of many social groups, for reasons that varied from case to case, including lack of opportunity as well as lack of recognition: most women, most people from outside Europe, most of the working class everywhere?

And yet the very idea of democracy depends upon a common social ethic, far beyond the minutiae of politics and constitutions, a set of common understandings about what society is, what it is aiming for, and how it relates to the autonomous life of individuals. Developing these understandings does require skills, but it also requires knowledge and ultimately wisdom. The old Arnoldian view of culture may have been imperfect, but, in rejecting it, we are close to rejecting any idea of a common culture altogether.

The key dilemma for us is then this. We are apparently agreed on the need for critical reflection. But, as we move rapidly away from the idea that a common education requires a common understanding of a standard body of knowledge – away from the importance of fostering cultural literacy – have we given up on the notion that critical capacities may be developed in a truly democratic way only if they are honed in the process of engaging with a cultural tradition?

Notes

1. Learning and Teaching Scotland, *Education for Citizenship in Scotland* (Dundee and Glasgow: LTS, 2002), p. 7; emphasis in the original.
2. Ibid.
3. L. Paterson and R. Bond, 'Higher education and critical citizenship: a survey of academics' views in Scotland and England', *Pedagogy, Culture and Society* 13 (2005), pp. 205–31 and R. Bond and L. Paterson, 'Coming down from the ivory tower? Academics' civic and economic engagement with the community', *Oxford Review of Education* 31 (2005), pp. 331–51; L. Paterson and R. Bond, 'Have Scottish academic

values been eroded?' *Scottish Affairs* 52 (2005), Summer, pp. 15–44.

4. For details of the material in the rest of this section, see L. Paterson, 'The modernising of the democratic intellect: the role of English in Scottish secondary education, 1900–1939', *Journal of Scottish Historical Studies* 24 (2004), pp. 45–79.

The Contribution of Religious Education to Citizenship

J. Mark Halstead

Although many writers simply take it for granted that there is a close connection between religious education and citizenship[1] and believe that the two subjects should coexist in a harmonious and mutually supportive relationship in schools, not everyone agrees. Some teachers, we are told, regard RE as virtually 'a synonym for citizenship',[2] but others 'want to build a fence between RE and Citizenship'[3] and view citizenship education with 'open hostility'.[4] Grimmitt sees citizenship as a direct threat to RE, potentially undermining 'the educational contribution that RE is making', and he suggests that 'this government, like the previous one, has little belief in RE's personal and community value'.[5] There may indeed be some grounds for Grimmitt's concern: the final report of the Advisory Group on Citizenship[6] makes only passing reference to RE, and Hargreaves (1994)[7] has called for citizenship education to replace RE in non-denominational schools.[8] Nevertheless, other educationalists have chosen to emphasise the 'vital and distinctive contribution' that RE can make to citizenship education[9] – a contribution based on the exploration of values and moral responsibility, the nature of commitment, allegiance and identity,[10] the beliefs and values of minority groups, the significance of community cohesion and many other key issues.

This disagreement is perhaps not surprising in view of the widely divergent attitudes to the very notion of citizenship that religious adherents may hold. Four main ways that believers think about citizenship can be distinguished:

1. Some believers choose to withdraw from involvement in the public domain of the state or the broader society, either literally as in the case of monks and nuns, or spiritually as in the case of the believer who sings 'This world is not my home, I'm just passing through'. Such believers consider themselves sojourners in a foreign land, and this view is reinforced by Jesus's saying, 'My kingdom is not of this world; else would my servants fight'.[11] For some Muslims, citizenship of a western state is doubly problematic – first because their primary loyalty in this life is to *dar al-Islam* (the land of Islam) rather than to any nation state, and second, because this life is in any case only a foretaste of and testing ground for the life to come. Muslims who take this view would rather follow the *shari'ah* than national laws, and would not consider it appropriate to fight for their country of residence against fellow-Muslims.
2. Other believers may seek total social and political involvement in the affairs of the state in which they live, in the belief that religious teaching is directly relevant to such political issues as human rights and social justice and that the believer has a moral duty to get involved in social action. On this view, believers should make their voice heard in elections and in the construction of the shared values of the broader society as well as actively campaigning on social issues. Muslims adopting this position would be more likely to acknowledge their nationality as central to

their identity, accept national laws, and fight for their country.

3. The third view is that the religious and the political are distinct but equally important dimensions of human existence, the one referring to issues of faith and the inner spiritual life and the other to public policy and public services. Both may involve duties ('Render to Caesar the things that are Caesar's and to God the things that are God's').[12] On this view, the recognition of a secular, civil framework of public values does not undermine or endanger loyalty to a faith community or the importance of religious identity, and communities have the right to lobby the political authorities in support of their own interests, including the freedom to live in accordance with the principles of their faith. From a Muslim perspective, however, this view is in tension with the Islamic doctrine of *tawhid* (the unity in all things and the supremacy of religion).
4. The fourth view is that religion is entirely a matter of individual choice. From a liberal perspective, individuals are free to follow their own wishes and inclinations in religion as in other areas of life, so long as the exercise of such freedom does not infringe the public interest or the equal right of all other human beings to the same freedoms. The state has no other interest in whether individuals are religious or not. This is probably the view that comes closest to the underlying assumptions of the final report of the Advisory Group on Citizenship,[13] and may partly explain why that report gave such scant attention to the contribution of RE to citizenship.

In this chapter,[14] I intend to provide a critical examination of the arguments for and against the use of RE as a vehicle for teaching at least some elements of citizenship, especially those relating to values, diversity and social cohesion. This involves examining the extent to which the content of RE and citizenship actually overlaps, the question whether the inclusion of citizenship issues in RE lessons is likely to alter the latter's essential character and purpose, and the extent to which (if at all) the teaching of citizenship makes RE redundant. The context of the discussion is the English education system, though it is hoped that the principles identified have much wider application. The chapter falls into four sections. The first provides a brief overview of contemporary English approaches to RE. The second examines the arguments in support of making close links between RE and citizenship. The third explores some of the practical approaches that may be adopted to give substance to the links. The fourth offers a critique of these links, and highlights some possible dangers in tying RE too closely to citizenship. The chapter concludes with reference to tensions that may exist between civic and religious identity.

Religious Education – Contemporary Approaches in England

When legislation was introduced in England and Wales twenty years ago to set up the National Curriculum for all state-funded schools, RE was not included as a National Curriculum subject. Nevertheless, it continues to be part of the basic curriculum that all schools are required to provide (along with a daily act of non-denominational collective worship) for all registered pupils, except for those whose parents specifically request their withdrawal from the provision. The reason for its exclusion from the National Curriculum was so that the curriculum could continue to be agreed at local rather than national level and thus take account of religious differences in different districts. However, there is a growing view among teachers and educational policy makers that the religious needs of children do not differ from place to place, and that a National Curriculum for religious education may be appropriate after all. Early moves towards this were made in October 2004 with the launch of the first non-statutory National Framework for Teaching Religious Education, and in September 2007 with the inclusion of religious education in the new secondary curriculum (due to start in schools in September 2008). Currently, however, the national framework merely provides guidelines for the development of locally Agreed Syllabuses, and it is the latter that carry the force of law.

Each locally Agreed Syllabus for Religious Education has since 1996 been required by law to reflect the fact that the religious traditions of the country are in the main Christian, while taking into account the teachings and practices of the other principal religions represented in the country. Non-compulsory schemes of work for RE have been produced by most LEAs to help schools to meet the requirements of their locally Agreed Syllabus, and these schemes of work typically fall into two main sections: learning *about* religion and religions, and learning *from* religions. The latter category covers such topics as values, commitments and questions of meaning, while the former involves several units on world faiths. For example, the publication *Schemes of Work for Religious Education in Devon, Plymouth and Torbay* has a major unit entitled 'How does Islam Provide a Complete Way of Life?' for Year 8 students (aged 12–13). The unit provides space to study Muslim beliefs and practices, and the way Islamic values impact on contemporary social, moral and political issues.[15]

RE in state-funded English community schools has thus changed dramatically over the last fifty years. The approach then was largely confessional, and the implicit aim was to encourage children to accept Christian principles and beliefs and in a sense to initiate them into the Christian faith. However, as English society became more multicultural and ethnically diverse, this approach gradually came to be seen as inappropriate, and a more multi-faith approach was adopted. Nowadays there is a stronger focus on understanding the nature and significance of religious faith, particularly in relation to contemporary ethical issues, and developing an understanding of the belief systems of six major world religions (Buddhism, Christianity, Hinduism, Islam, Judaism and Sikhism). The approach is usually phenomenological and the aims are to encourage intercommunity understanding and to facilitate personal choice about religion. As Robert Jackson points out, RE is now 'both critical and reflective ... The ethical teachings of religions and spiritual movements are thus source material for study and reflection rather than sources of authority which all pupils are expected to follow'.[16] Because the approach is non-confessional and concerned with developing an *understanding* of religion rather than a *commitment* to it, comparatively few parents exercise their right to withdraw their children from RE.

RE has traditionally been a low-status subject that many students do not take seriously.[17] Somewhat surprisingly, however, the subject has recently been experiencing something of a revival, particularly as a GCSE subject. This is perhaps because its open approach and relevance to life in multicultural Britain appeal to students, and also because it has shown that it can involve young people both intellectually and emotionally in open engagement with issues of truth, morality and the meaning of life.

Arguments for Links between the Two Subjects

We are now in a position to review the links that can be developed between RE and citizenship. The links, and the arguments in support of them that are set out below, have been explored in a range of recent publications.[18] They focus mainly on common concerns and subject matter that is relevant to both subjects.

1. Many commentators argue that both RE and citizenship are centrally concerned with attitudes and values. It has already been noted that with the demise of the confessional approach to RE, the contribution that RE makes to the development of students' values now has more to do with providing opportunities to discuss and reflect on the search for meaning and purpose in life and with encouraging the growth of tolerance, understanding and respect in our increasingly multicultural and multi-faith society.[19] These correspond closely to some of the values highlighted as central to citizenship in the final report of the Advisory Group on Citizenship. Arthur and Wright extend the list of core RE values when they claim that RE provides opportunities for pupils to 'understand the idea of duty and responsibility; develop positive relationships and friendships; explore the meaning of conflict; broaden their self-awareness and knowledge; enhance their potential for membership of strong communities; and understand the importance of shared values within community'.[20] For the National Curriculum Council, RE's contribution to the understanding of values is 'too obvious to merit discussion'.[21]
2. Both RE and citizenship are concerned with preparing students for the opportunities and responsibilities of adult life and with provision for their spiritual, moral, social and cultural development.[22] Though it is now widely accepted that religion and morality are logically distinct ways of interpreting experience,[23] religions still often provide a source for moral vision and it is not surprising that for many years RE has been regarded

as a 'major vehicle for moral education'.[24] It is in RE that students are most likely to be introduced to ethical issues like euthanasia, medical ethics, animal rights, sexual ethics, environmental ethics, the treatment of refugees and asylum seekers and world poverty.

3. Religion provides a major form of community involvement for many pupils, and can thus become a major resource for learning about community engagement. Keast notes that, through RE, pupils will not only visit nearby faith communities and use them as a resource for learning, but will also come to understand their role in developing young people's commitments and identity and their contribution to community cohesion and inclusion.[25] Through such insights into issues of commitment, identity, diversity and community involvement, RE can make a significant contribution to developing informed citizens.

4. Ipgrave[26] notes that religion is also an area of public/civic concern, because of communal tensions and the prejudice, discrimination and exclusion that can emerge out of religious ignorance.[27] Both national issues like the 2001 riots, the activities of the British National Party, and the segregation of religious communities, and international issues like 9/11, the Palestinian problem and the Danish cartoons form part of many students' political awareness. Ipgrave found that children often make links between religious issues and citizenship and her research shows children introducing 'the language of religion into that of communal relations' and also bringing 'knowledge of political procedures into their considerations of religion'.[28]

5. It is sometimes claimed that both RE and citizenship can provide opportunities for students to develop generic skills like enquiry, debate and communication

and more specific skills like empathy, critical reflection and the capacity to deal with bias.[29] In view of what Tobler calls the 'glaring gender-blindness in modern citizenship theory',[30] the development of critical reflection through RE and citizenship may be particularly important for young people.

6. Finally, both RE and citizenship have a shared potential for contributing to students' learning about diversity and pluralism. Citizenship requires all children to learn about different ethnic and religious identities in Britain today, and since students are taught in RE about the beliefs, values and practices of all the major religious traditions in the country, it is assumed that RE meets the requirements of citizenship in this respect. Ipgrave offers one example, an inter-faith e-mail project that was set up between schools in Leicester and East Sussex explicitly to address the shared concerns of RE and citizenship regarding diversity.[31]

On the basis of this overlapping subject matter and these shared purposes, Keast argues that where citizenship is taught as a discrete subject in schools, RE teachers should at least be involved in its planning and evaluation, and where it is taught through a more cross-curricular approach, RE teachers should be even more closely involved in its delivery.[32]

Practical Links

This section provides an overview of possible links between citizenship and RE, particularly with reference to recent Qualifications and Curriculum Authority (QCA) documents and schemes of work, and illustrates some practical approaches where citizenship can be enriched by a contribution from RE.[33] In fact, RE and citizenship are often taught by the same teachers in secondary schools, and RE Agreed Syllabuses often contain sections on citizenship.[34] According to the QCA document 'Citizenship through Religious Education at Key Stage 3',[35] pupils need to learn 'how individual, group and political choices, policies and actions' are influenced by and 'inextricably linked with … religious and moral beliefs, practices and values'. RE can help children understand 'personal, social and moral responsibility' and to consider how human beings treat each other and their environments. Further, RE can help 'to develop active citizenship by involvement with voluntary religious and charitable activities'.[36]

Some more examples from this QCA report may be helpful to give a brief flavour of the possible synergy between RE and citizenship. In citizenship, 'legal and human rights and responsibilities' (1a) can be supported in RE when religious people who have promoted human rights, such as Martin Luther King, are studied. In one lesson where children were asked to consider whether various actions were right or wrong, the class were unanimous that adultery was morally wrong but something approaching a moment of revelation was witnessed when they realised that the state did not punish everything they considered to be wrong. This then led onto a discussion of whether the state should intervene in what are viewed as private, family matters and the realisation that legality and morality are not the same in the twenty-first century.[37] Nevertheless, children need to learn that many laws have religious origins and that in the UK the Christian roots of many laws are still apparent today.

When looking at the 'work of community-based, national and international voluntary groups' (1f), children can consider the role of religious aid agencies such as Islamic Relief and Christian Aid and can listen to speakers from such organisations as the Salvation Army which work with alcoholics and homeless people. When considering the significance of the media in society (1h), students can study the portrayal of different religious figures in the media (compare the portrayal of the Dalai Lama and the Rev. Sun Myung Moon). In citizenship, children are required to use their imagination 'to consider other people's experiences' and to 'explain views that are not their own' (3a) and this fits well with current approaches to RE where children are encouraged to see an issue from the perspective of adherents of different religions. Indeed, it would be difficult to think about 'topical political, spiritual, moral, social and cultural issues' (2a) without understanding and responding to religious teachings and paying heed to the nature of values and beliefs.

A Critique of the Links between Teaching RE and Citizenship

The study of religion clearly has much to offer citizenship, and the areas that RE and citizenship have in common (as we have seen) are reasonably easy to identify, though there is a danger in making claims that are too extravagant. Keast, for example, when discussing the biblical command to 'love your neighbour', argues that questions like what it means to love our neighbours are both religious questions and citizenship issues.[38] But this is precisely not the case. Respecting one's neighbour's rights or treating him with social justice may well be citizenship issues, but not *loving* him. This is a spiritual, not a civic response. Still less is 'loving God' a citizenship issue, though understanding people who believe that this is the ultimate meaning of life may be (ibid.). What is more complex than merely identifying areas of overlap, however, is the task of discerning the impact upon each subject of the ways in which the other is generally formulated and taught in state schools. This is the task we must turn to now. In this section, two issues in particular will be discussed: the attitudes of the two subjects to cultural and religious diversity, and the problematic nature of 'learning from religion' in the context of citizenship.

Tolerating or Celebrating Diversity

The programmes of study for National Curriculum Citizenship include the requirement for students to be taught about 'the diversity of national, regional, religious and ethnic identities in the United Kingdom and the need for mutual respect and understanding', and to be taught to 'use their imagination to consider other people's experiences and be able to think about, express and explain views that are not their own'.[39] The contribution that RE can make here is clear and self-evident, and it is all the more surprising that the final report of the Advisory Group on Citizenship ignores it completely. Watson's view is that the report's authors appear to have a totally different response to diversity from that of religious educationalists.[40] The National Framework for Religious Education states that RE 'places specific emphasis on ... the *celebration* of diversity in society',[41] whereas the AGC Report identifies cultural diversity as a matter of concern and suggests that finding 'a sense of common citizenship, including a national identity' is the best way of 'responding to these worries'.[42] Insofar as the AGC represents current thinking on the topic, Watson is surely right to point out that

> the gap between citizenship education and religious education is potentially enormous with each subject taking politically divergent routes to addressing the challenge of British cultural and worldview pluralism. Citizenship education appears to equate with a conformity to one-nation values, while religious education celebrates diversity and encourages dialogue.[43]

Two points emerge from this. The first is that RE does indeed have an enriching contribution to make to citizenship by welcoming and facilitating dialogue between different faiths and cultures. The second is that RE may need to be wary of too close an involvement with citizenship, because the goals and aspirations of the two subjects are not the same, and RE's primary purposes of developing open-mindedness and respect for all, engaging with the meaning and purpose of life, celebrating diversity and exploring ethics in a global context may provide an important alternative framework of values to those espoused by some of the main proponents of citizenship education.

Learning from Religion

If RE does have a significant contribution to make to citizenship, this seems to fall under the heading of the attainment target, 'learning from religion'.[44] The phrase 'learning from religion' indicates a particular approach where religious activity and belief is related to 'common human experience'. It is described in the following terms:

> Pupils should be able to make clear links between *common human experiences* and what religious people believe and do. Rituals, festivals, rites of passage, beliefs about God and the world – all these connect with *common human experiences* of awe, celebration, passage of time, a quest for meaning, purpose and value. *Learning from religion* requires pupils to see how such experiences are understood and interpreted in varying ways by members of different faiths and by those without religious beliefs.[45]

While this would seem *prima facie* to be in harmony with the requirement in the National Curriculum citizenship programmes of study that students should be taught to 'think about topical political, spiritual, moral, social and cultural issues, problems and events' and 'justify orally and in writing a personal opinion about such issues',[46] this may present some specific problems at the point where RE and citizenship meet. Attempting to make a particular religion relevant to those who are not adherents can be helpful but also deeply problematic, not least because the focus on response and applying religious belief to a child's everyday secular experience can lead to the trivialisation of a religion.

Thompson[47] distinguishes between 'extraction' and 'distraction' methods of learning from religion. In the 'extraction' method an idea that is not central is taken out of context. For instance, a lesson on Moses' leadership qualities might be the focus of attention when the burning bush, the Exodus and giving of Ten Commandments are taught, so that the religious message of the stories becomes secularised into a story about leadership. But the 'distraction' method is perhaps more dangerous, for in the attempt to make religion relevant, the original meaning may be deeply confused. For example, when teaching the five pillars of Islam, non-Muslim children might be encouraged to relate these pillars to their own lives. They complete the sentence 'One month each year for self-discipline Muslims ...' and then they are asked to finish off a parallel sentence 'My ambition for the next year is ...' in a misguided attempt to make Muslim behaviour comprehensible. In this case:

> Attention is immediately taken off Muslims and the possibility of children taking their faith seriously, and put onto matters which have little relation to the Muslim equivalent. What relation has naked ambition to the self-discipline required of a Muslim?[48]

The QCA states that 'the GCSE short course has moved awarding bodies towards greater attention to religion as a meaning-making activity, that is, *learning from religion*'.[49] But Wright warns us to be wary of any approaches to RE which simply induct pupils 'into the rules of the post-modern game, encouraging them to construct their own realities, on the basis of unrestrained freedom, desire, will and preference'.[50] Such approaches cannot be justified as the best way to develop tolerance and respect for others. Little is to be gained from obscuring doctrinal differences between Muslims and Christians, for example. Muslims and Christians can disagree on the nature of Jesus and still agree on the importance of the rule of law and the moral duty to live peaceably together. To encourage children to engage with such truth claims is valuable in citizenship for it promotes a judicious understanding of the beliefs of others while recognising that tolerance is not based on agreement but can be promoted by an awareness of differences.

Conclusion

At the heart of citizenship lies the search for shared values and a shared understanding of what it is to be a member of a liberal democratic society. At the heart of RE (as it is currently conceived in the West) lies an appreciation of diverse faiths and an understanding of spiritual and moral values and commitments. These two sets of central concerns may touch at certain points, especially their interest in issues of equality, diversity, tolerance and respect, but their focus of attention is different; for example, the civic virtues promoted through citizenship[51] are different from the religious virtues to which children are introduced in RE. Both subjects prepare children for life in a multicultural society, but while RE stresses the diverse beliefs, values and identities that make a society multicultural, citizenship tends to emphasise the common elements that make a multicultural society a single society. The more diverse a society is, the more effort has to be put into any attempts to create an underlying unity and cohesion. As Blaylock points out, any society needs its shared narratives,[52] and the introduction of citizenship into the National Curriculum is itself part of this search for unity and cohesion. So are citizenship tests, the plan to create a special English Day, the proposed citizenship ceremonies and so on – innovations that suggest England is determined to learn from America's use of civil religion (such as saluting the flag at the start of the school day) as a unifying force (Bellah 1967).[53]

Few people would wish to argue with the claim that schools have a responsibility to prepare young people for citizenship in a democratic, pluralist society and, as part of this, to develop a respectful and sympathetic understanding of beliefs and worldviews they do not share. The study of religion can clearly contribute to this (as can the study of diverse forms of literature, art, music and other aspects of culture), particularly if believers are not stereotyped as conforming totally to a fixed group identity and a pre-packaged and unchanging framework of beliefs and practices. But a problem remains for some believers (and not only those mentioned earlier who seek to minimise their involvement in the public domain), particularly if teaching about religious diversity is encouraged for purely secular purposes, if it is assumed that one's primary identity must always be defined in terms of national rather than religious allegiance, and if the 'public' values of citizenship are always given priority over the 'private' values of religion. For these believers there is a real fear that in the name of (the liberal values of) social cohesion, public neutrality and non-indoctrination, key spiritual and moral values may be undermined and children may find themselves, intentionally or otherwise, encouraged to turn away from the distinctive beliefs of their family and community. These fears feed the continuing demand for faith schools in some quarters. But if citizenship is to fulfil its potential for promoting social cohesion, its proponents must be prepared to reassure those who continue to have doubts. Faith schools need not be dismissed as isolationist or divisive, but can be seen as symbols of a healthy multiculturalism and equality of respect. It is only if inter-group dialogue and communication are encouraged and students are free to explore their own identities in a critical, reflective and open way (whether in faith schools or community schools) that collaboration between RE and citizenship will be seen as positive and successful.

Notes

1. John Keast, 'Religious, moral and spiritual education and citizenship: managing and building on the interface', in Tony Breslin and Barry Dufour (eds), *Developing Citizens* (London: Hodder Murray, 2006), p. 301.
2. Alan Brown and Erica Brown, 'Religious Education', in Stephen Bigger and Erica Brown (eds), *Spiritual, Moral, Social and Cultural Education: exploring values in the curriculum* (London: David Fulton, 1999), p. 17.
3. Lat Blaylock (ed.), *Secondary RE and Citizenship: towards an open frontier* (Birmingham: Christian Education Publications, 2002), p. 2.
4. Jacqueline Watson, 'Educating for Citizenship – the emerging relationship between religious education and citizenship education', *British Journal of Religious Education* 26, 3 (2004), p. 262.
5. Michael Grimmitt, *Pedagogies of Religious Education* (Great Wakering: McCrimmon, 2000), p. 11.
6. B. Crick, *Education for Citizenship and the Teaching of Democracy in Schools: Final Report of the Advisory Group on Citizenship* (London: QCA, 1998).
7. David Hargreaves, *The Mosaic of Learning: schools and teachers for the next century* (London: Demos, 1994).
8. For a fuller discussion of Hargreaves' arguments, see Robert Jackson, *International Perspectives on Citizenship, Education and Religious Diversity* (London: Routledge Falmer, 2003), ch. 4.
9. Robert Jackson, 'Editorial: religious education and education for citizenship', *British Journal of Religious Education* 24, 3 (2002), p. 162.
10. Keast, 2006, p. 301.
11. John 18:36.
12. Mark 12:17.
13. B. Crick, 1998.
14. This chapter is an expansion and development of some reflections first set out in chapter 7 of my book *Citizenship*

and Moral Education: values in action (London: Routledge, 2006), and I want to express my thanks to my co-author, Mark Pike.

15. Devon County Council, The Devon, Plymouth and Torbay Agreed Syllabus for Religious Education (Exeter: Devon County Council, 2001).
16. Jackson, 2003, p. 18.
17. Monica Taylor, 'Voicing their values: pupils' moral and cultural experience', in Mark Halstead and Monica Taylor (eds), *Values in Education and Education in Values* (London: Falmer Press, 1996), p. 127.
18. Vivienne Baumfield, 'Democratic RE: preparing young people for citizenship', *British Journal of Religious Education* 25, 3 (2003), pp. 173–84; Lat Blaylock (ed.), *Secondary RE and Citizenship: towards an open frontier* (Birmingham: Christian Education Publications, 2002); Lynn Broadbent, 'Values education, citizenship and the contribution of RE', in R. Bailey (ed.), *Teaching Values and Citizenship across the Curriculum: educating children for the world* (London: RoutledgeFalmer, 2004); Pamela Draycott (ed.), *Primary RE and Citizenship* (Birmingham: Christian Education, 2002); Liam Gearon, *Citizenship through Secondary Religious Education* (London: RoutledgeFalmer, 2004); Jackson, 2002, 2003; Keast, 2006; Nick Mead, 'Researching skills common to Religious Education and Citizenship,' in Suzi Clipson-Boyles (ed.), *Putting Research into Practice in Primary Teaching and Learning* (London: Fulton, 2000); Jenny Pestridge (ed.), *Citizens of Faith: making a difference* (Birmingham: Christian Education Publications, 2002); Geoff Teece, 'Citizenship education and religious education: threat or opportunity?' *Resource: Journal of the Professional Council for RE* 21, 1 (1998), pp. 7–10; Watson, 2004.
19. Cf. Monica Taylor, 'Religious Education, Values and Worship: LEA advisers' perspectives on the implementation of the Education Reform Act in 1988' (Slough: NFER, 1989).
20. James Arthur and Daniel Wright, *Teaching Citizenship in the Secondary School* (London: David Fulton, 2001), p. 29.
21. National Curriculum Council, *The Whole Curriculum* (Curriculum Guidance 3), (York: NCC, 1990), p. 2.
22. Cf. Taylor, 1989.
23. Paul Hirst, *Moral Education in a Secular Society* (London: Hodder & Stoughton, 1974).

24. Jack Priestley, 'Comic role or cosmic vision? Religious Education and the teaching of values', in John Thacker, Richard Pring and David Evans (eds), *Personal, Social and Moral Education in a Changing World* (Windsor: NFER-Nelson, 1987), p. 107.
25. Keast, 2006, pp. 302–4.
26. Julia Ipgrave, 'Dialogue, citizenship and religious education', in Robert Jackson (ed.), *International Perspectives on Citizenship, Education and Religious Diversity* (London: RoutledgeFalmer, 2003), pp. 156ff.
27. Blaylock, 2002, p. 209.
28. Ipgrave, 2003, p. 158.
29. Keast, 2006, p. 304; Jackson, 2003, pp. 78–9.
30. Judy Tobler, 'Learning the difference: religious education, citizenship and gendered subjectivity', in Robert Jackson (ed.), *International perspectives on citizenship, education and religious diversity* (London: RoutledgeFalmer, 2003), p. 125.
31. Ipgrave, 2003, p. 154.
32. Keast, 2006, p. 303.
33. See also Keast, 2006, pp. 303–8 and Gearon, 2004 for further ideas.
34. Cf. Devon County Council, 2001, pp. 26–8.
35. Qualifications and Curriculum Authority, *Citizenship through Religious Education at Key Stage 3* (London: QCA, 2001).
36. Ibid., p. 1.
37. I am grateful to Mark Pike for this example.
38. Keast, 2006, p. 301.
39. Qualifications and Curriculum Authority/Department for Education and Employment, *Citizenship – The National Curriculum for England* (London: QCA, 1999), pp. 14–15.
40. Watson, 2004, p. 266.
41. Qualifications and Curriculum Authority, Personal, Social and Health Education: 2002–3 annual report on curriculum and assessment (London: QCA, 2004), p. 8, my italics.
42. AGC, 1998, p. 17.
43. Watson, 2004, p. 267.
44. QCA, 2004, pp. 33–7.
45. QCA, 2000, p. 23, my italics.
46. QCA/DfEE, 1999, p. 14.
47. Penny Thompson, *Whatever Happened to Religious Education?* (Cambridge: Lutterworth Press, 2004).
48. Ibid., p. 128.
49. QCA, 2000, p. 27, my italics.

50. Andrew Wright, 'The child in relationship: towards a communal model of spirituality', in Ron Best (ed.), *Education, Spirituality and the Whole Child* (London: Cassell, 1996), p. 144.
51. Pat White, *Civic Virtues and Public Schooling: educating citizens for a democratic society* (New York: Teachers College Press, 1996).
52. Blaylock, 2002, p. 209.
53. Robert Bellah, 'Civil religion in America', *Daedalus* 96, Winter (1967), pp. 1–21.

Growing Scientific Citizens in a High-tech World

Wilson Poon

Introduction

A few years ago, a number of Edinburgh University academics and their associates produced an admirable source book for citizenship education, *Renewing Democracy in Scotland.*[1] The list of contributors was impressively broad, ranging across seven of the University's (then) eight faculties, with the exception of the Faculty of Science and Engineering. This absence is odd. In today's world, science and technology daily presents us with conundrums and choices, so that an educated citizen must know how to make informed judgements about these.

Indeed, while none of the contributors to *Renewing Democracy in Scotland* was from the Faculty of Science and Engineering, the importance of technology for citizenship education was explicitly acknowledged by Tom Conlon (from the Faculty of Education): '(It) is clear that technology impinges upon major areas of policy including health, ecology and equality. Increasingly, technology issues are coming to the fore of political debate.'[2] Conlon defined technology as 'the application of science to change some aspect of the environment'. This model of the relationship between science and technology is very commonly held, but presents a one-sided picture. A more nuanced understanding of the differing nature of science and technology and how they relate to each other is vital to growing scientific citizens in today's high-tech world.

Technology is Doing and Science is Understanding

'Technology' (Greek *techne* = 'art' or 'skill'[3]) is about getting things done, and includes not only the traditional engineering disciplines (building bridges, aeroplanes, computers, etc.), but also medicine and agriculture. Its goal is power: 'Look, I can do that!' 'Science' (Latin *scientia* = 'knowledge') is about understanding how things work. Its goal is insight: 'Aha, I see!' Today, science and technology are symbiotic, but such intimacy is historically recent, and requires explanation. Technology is as ancient as humanity, while science as we know it is not much more than 400 years old.

The ancient origin of technology is attested across the globe by traditional stories that reach back to time immemorial. Chinese mythology features demi-gods such as *Shénnóng*, literally, 'divine farmer', and *Shuìrèn*, literally, 'stove man'. Interestingly, *Shénnóng* embodies the fantasy of risk-free technology. While tasting plants for edibility and medicinal properties he poisoned himself multiple times, but survived because he was semi-divine! *Shuìrèn* plays the role of Prometheus in Greek mythology, introducing fire to humans. In the Hebrew bible we read of Cain's descendants Jabal and Tubal-cain originating animal husbandry and metal working respectively (Genesis 4:20–2).

These ancient stories witness that in most of history, technology has *not* been 'the application of science to change some aspect of the environment': there simply was no science to apply! In contrast, modern science has made use of the latest technology from its inception. Galileo's telescope depended on new lens-grinding know-how. Demobilised scientists from the Second World War built the first radio telescopes using surplus radar equipment. Today's particle physicists rely on complex accelerators and detectors. Some scholars suggest that such a 'technological bias' determines the very nature of modern science. Thus, the philosopher Amos Funkenstein contrasts a *contemplative* medieval natural philosophy, whose goal was edification, with an *ergetic* (Greek *ergos* = work) modern science: a *knowing by doing* that equates understanding with the ability to reconstruct.[4]

Consider two contemporary sciences in this light. Inside particle accelerators, physicists can recreate the conditions of the first few seconds of the Big Bang, yielding an 'ergetic' understanding of nothing less than the universe itself. The implicit goal of biology, at least since the discovery of the DNA double helix, is the recreation of life from inorganic materials. The rise of the new discipline of 'synthetic biology', and Craig Venter's recent headline-grabbing synthesis of the smallest possible single-cell organism supposedly 'from scratch', merely bring this hitherto largely unspoken 'ergetic' goal of biology into the open: if we can recreate life, then we can truly claim to understand it.

I find Funkenstein convincing. If he is right, then modern science was 'born in bed with technology'. In turn, as the philosopher Carl Mitcham has suggested, 'it is precisely the inherently technological character of science that makes technology in the modern sense possible'.[5] But the birth of modern technology needed one more ingredient: the professionalisation of science. Friederich Wilhelm von Humboldt founded the first modern research university in Berlin in 1810. Henceforth, professional 'scientists', a word coined by William Whewell (Master of Trinity College, Cambridge) in 1834, are paid to work in laboratories to enquire systematically into the workings of the world (science), which vastly increases our ability to get things done (technology). The symbiosis between electronics and solid-state physics is a paradigmatic example. Because we understand electrical conduction in semiconductors very well, synthetic materials can be designed for particular applications (e.g. multicolour light-emitting diodes). So, while humans have always lived with technology, the latter's symbiosis with science has brought about modern *high* technology, characterised by complexity, global reach and rapid change. In such a world, many scientists work as technologists.

Technology Involves Inevitable Risks

The close alliance between modern science and technology may spawn an illusion: that science can deliver risk-free technology. We have already met this fantasy in *Shénnóng*. Today, we have exchanged a demi-god for a white-coated scientist. In either case, we want power without risk. This fantasy is illustrated by an interview I heard on BBC Radio 4 at the height of the controversy concerning a possible link between the triple mumps, measles and rubella vaccination (a new medical technology) and autism. The interviewer asked a scientist whether he could guarantee that the triple vaccine was 'absolutely safe', i.e. 'as safe as aspirin'. For this interviewer, science should be the guarantor of risk-free technology. But this is not possible, because (a) power and understanding are asymmetrically related, and (b) complex systems are chaotic and non-linear.

Consider first the asymmetric relation between power and understanding. While in 'ergetic' science there is no understanding without (re)construction, the converse is untrue. Even in an era of rapid scientific progress, construction (technology) is entirely possible, and indeed likely, without complete understanding (science). Consider Dolly the Sheep (5/7/96–14/2/03). Almost none of the steps in the cloning process are understood even today. For instance, it's unclear why a pulse of electricity could fuse two cells; but it *does* work, sometimes. The accumulated ignorance over some 100 procedures is reflected in the low overall success rate, and in unanticipated effects such as premature aging. Dolly the Sheep is a technological, rather than scientific, breakthrough. A lot of scientific knowledge certainly went into Dolly, and most of the people involved were trained as scientists. But the project was a technological one aimed at making cloning work and (ultimately) using it for other technological ends (such as organ transplantation).[6]

Dolly illustrates how a single technological advance can create multiple puzzles (and indeed, opportunities) for scientists. On the other hand, every advance in 'ergetic' science is technological (a successful re*construction* of something or other), which in turn may yield further technological opportunities. In this scenario of technology spawning science which spawns technology, there simply isn't any hope of understanding (science) ever keeping up with doing (technology), so that the latter will inevitably be risky.

Another risk generator is complexity. A complex system is made up of many interacting components. The planets in the solar system and the sun all gravitationally tugging each other, a bucket of water with over a trillion trillion molecules bouncing off and attracting each other, the cells in a human body communicating via nerve impulses and hormones, the millions of computers in the worldwide web exchanging information, and the stockbrokers on a trading floor second-guessing each other's minds are examples. Complex systems have two features that render them risky to manipulate: chaos and non-linearity.

First, complex systems may show chaotic behaviour, i.e., very small uncertainties in the input parameters used to model them can give rise to dramatic uncertainties in the predicted outcomes. A butterfly flapping its wings in Brazil may turn balmy sunshine into squally showers in London. Second, the response of complex systems to perturbations can be highly non-linear. Heat up some water at room temperature by 0.1°C, and its volume will increase a little (a few thousandth of a per cent). Such 'sensible' response continues until 99.9°C; then you get a shock – the volume increases by more than a thousandfold in response to the next 0.1°C rise – the water boils and becomes steam. Stock-market crashes in response to changing economic conditions[7] and the possible abrupt cessation of the Gulf Stream in response to global warming are other examples of non-linearity in complex systems. In such systems, the last straw can indeed break the camel's back – and we do not always know where such 'critical points' are lurking.

Educating Citizens about Risk

To summarise, the asymmetric relation between technology and science together with the nature of complex systems mean that *technology is inevitably risky*. Grasping this point is essential in a society that is increasingly risk-adverse. This is illustrated by a comment from the outgoing chairman of a major pharmaceutical company interviewed on BBC Radio 4, who opined that had aspirin been invented today, it would never have been licensed. This common painkiller probably has more known side effects than any other drug licensed today. Most of these were discovered through continual use since 1899 rather than predicted by pharmacological science. Interestingly, many 'side effects' can be harnessed for non-analgesic clinical purposes (e.g. thinning blood after heart attacks). So aspirin, while not 'absolutely safe', is indeed one of the safest drugs, *not* because it has no side effects, but because many of its side effects are known and some are even understood. Importantly, such safety for us today comes from previous generations taking risks on our behalf.

Take another example, the bicycle, a form of 'green' transport that we are increasingly encouraged to (re)turn to. Perhaps surprisingly, physicists are still not agreed why the complex mechanical system of bicycle-plus-rider should stay upright. Moreover, in road trials, a fraction of riders would undoubtedly fall off, and other safety concerns abound, e.g. risks from cars. I doubt that 'low-carbon bi-pedal transporters' would ever be licensed for general public use today! As it is, many generations of users have demonstrated convincingly that humans-on-bicycles can be stable, and have trained us to take on the other associated risks.

These two 'thought experiments' show that for society to continue to benefit from technological advances, each generation must take risks for subsequent generations. We urgently need informed public debate and democratic consensus on the degree of such risks that we want to take on as a society, and how we deal with the consequences. To achieve this, citizens need an appreciation of the scale of risks already involved in everyday activities that we all do with little thought, and an understanding of 'the rules of chance'.

Concerning everyday risks, Richard Wilson has helpfully tabulated activities that would increase the chance of death by one in a million in the year 1979 (i.e. if 1 million people all engaged in the activity, one extra death would result), e.g. cycling ten miles (from traffic accident), flying 1,000 miles (from accidents) or 6,000 miles (cancer from exposure to cosmic radiation), and drinking two-thirds of a bottle of wine (from liver cirrhosis).[8] Weighing everyday risks helps to put any new technological risks into perspective.

To see the importance of understanding 'the rules of chance', consider 'cancer clusters', putative cancer 'hot spots' associated with some local technology (e.g. a mobile phone base station mast). The epidemiological issues are complex and each case has unique features. But one question is vital in all cases: if cancer strikes at random, what is the likelihood of the observed cluster showing up purely by chance?

Answering this question is non-trivial; e.g. one has to consider age variations across different regions. But a simpler example illustrates the essential point. Eyewitnesses to German V2 rocket attacks on London in the Second World War repeatedly claimed that the bombs were targeted at particular areas. To test this hypothesis, a scientist[9] divided a 144 km^2 area of south London where 537 rockets landed into 576 squares of ¼ km^2 each, and counted the hits in each square. Since there is an average of 0.932 hits per square, 'common sense' may expect that a non-targeted, 'random' shower of bombs should lead to most squares (say, about 90 per cent) taking a single hit, with a few (say, about 10 per cent) taking no hits. The real situation is shown below, together with the expected distribution of bombs calculated assuming that they fall randomly.

No. of bombs per square	*Actual no. of squares*	*Expected no. of squares*
0	229	226.74
1	211	211.39
2	93	98.54
3	35	30.62
4	7	7.14
5 and over	1	1.57
	576	576.00

The measured distribution bears no resemblance to 'common sense', but follows the 'random-hit' model, which predicts that, strikingly, nearly 40 per cent of the squares take *no* hits, while nearly 7 per cent take three hits or more. One can see why residents reasoning from 'common sense' might have thought that the Germans were aiming at particular targets, especially when those in high-hit neighbourhoods compared notes with those (the majority!) whose neighbourhoods sustained no hit. But postwar investigations show that they were wrong.

The moral is that a completely random process can naturally give rise to 'clusters'. More generally, this example shows that 'common sense' can easily lead us astray when it comes to assessing chance and risk. Thus, when epidemiologists repeat this kind of analysis for cancer clusters, they often find that there is no evidence to bear out 'cancer hot spot' theories, i.e. the observed clusters are entirely compatible with chance. Nevertheless, the public seldom believe them.[10] No doubt, this is partly due to the well-entrenched 'common sense' approach to chance already noted. But it may also reveal a misunderstanding of what science is, and what and how fast it can deliver.

The Scientific Process Takes Time

The word *science* refers to a loose collection of methodologies and processes for generating reliable knowledge about the material world,[11] and to the body of knowledge so generated. Science education has traditionally focused on the latter. For citizenship education, the former is far more important. I say 'a loose collection', because different sciences use methods appropriate to their subject matter. Studying historical processes such as biological evolution or galaxy formation, where laboratory experiments are seldom possible, requires reasoning distinctive from semiconductor physics, where laboratory experiments are routine. 'Big science' (astronomy, particle physics), relying on large teams and giant facilities, functions quite differently from 'small' laboratory-based sciences.

In 'small science', a team typically consisting of an established researcher, a couple of postdoctoral research assistants and a number of PhD students tackles a problem, seeking results within the period of a competitively-awarded grant, typically three years. When results emerge, they will write it up and submit the manuscript to a scientific journal. After weeks to months, the authors receive comments from anonymous 'referees'– fellow scientists whom the journal editor has asked to evaluate the work. The refereeing process is quite conservative: breakthroughs are often repeatedly rejected. If the authors can persuade the referees, the paper will eventually be published. After the paper is noticed, read and digested, which can take months to years, others will start using its results to build their own projects. The typical 'lead time' in applying for and getting new grants is a year or more. The cycle then repeats. Irreproducible data are eventually forgotten, over-hasty theories are replaced by more solid models, and our understanding of a particular problem is gradually refined.[12]

This process *does* generate reliable knowledge (see Ziman's book of that title), *but it takes time*. As a rule of thumb, consensus is reached over a decade or longer, and the road to this point is tortuous, necessarily littered with false leads, flawed experiments, incomplete data, etc. (It took four years to identify the AIDS virus, and five more to understand it enough for the first effective 'combination therapy' to emerge.) In the process, scientists will argue and disagree with one another repeatedly. Sometimes, after lengthy investigation, the community may even decide that consensus is not yet possible, and collectively 'ditch' the subject for the time being.

The 'natural scientific cycle' appears slow for the non-specialist. I remember a senior scientist in charge of one of the UK's main science funding councils being interviewed on BBC Radio 4 concerning a case of scientific fraud by a Korean stem-cell researcher. The interviewer wanted to know why 'it took so long' for the fraud to be discovered. The scientist pointed out that the timescale concerned, seven months, was actually amazingly short in terms of the 'natural scientific cycle'!

Thus, when society gives a problem to science (e.g. 'Can BSE jump the species barrier?'), it is completely unrealistic to expect science to come up with anything approaching a consensus answer on the timescale of months or even a few years, however much public money is poured in. Unfortunately, many appear to expect precisely such quick results, and end up repeatedly disappointed. They then conclude that science does not have a useful contribution to make. But that would be throwing the proverbial baby out with the bathwater. The right thing to do is to learn collectively how to use uncertain science-in-the-making in the public arena.

Space precludes discussion of this important subject, but an excellent recent volume is available.[13] Instead, I note that it is important not to let current scientific uncertainty cloud our perception of what science *can* confidently offer. For instance, scientists understand the relevant systems well enough to say quite certainly that:

- Rampant use of antibiotics *will* give rise to rapid acquisition of drug resistance among microbes (although the detailed mechanisms are still far from fully understood);
- As the globe continues to warm, at some point ocean currents *will* change abruptly giving rise to dramatic climatic consequences (although there is somewhat less consensus on precisely when that point will come and what the consequences may be, but progress is rapid in this area).

These two items illustrate well that it is often not the lack of knowledge that impedes reasoned public decision-making!

Conclusion: Technology, Science and Society

There is no doubt that thinking about science and technology is a key part of citizenship education. The modern symbiosis between these two areas of human endeavour has brought tremendous benefits: the life expectancy in the UK has nearly doubled (from 40 to nearly 80) since Whewell coined the word 'scientist'; over the same period, the price of wheat has dropped by a factor of ten.[14] Technological advances, often enabled by science, have also brought problems, local and global, ethical and political. Citizens should be involved in making decisions about how to continue to reap the benefits responsibly while minimising, or even eliminating, the harms. Science has also brought significant cultural gains. That we now wash hands rather than sacrifice children to avert infectious epidemics is partly due to the growth of the scientific worldview. Society needs to learn how to foster the conditions under which science can continue to thrive. It is salutary to note that the immediate previous president of the Royal Society, Lord May, chose to use his final annual presidential address (2005) to warn of the threat posed by religious fundamentalism to science. I should simply add that science in fact withers under extremisms of all kinds: a militant *scientism* that insists on scientific rationality being the only rationality is just as bad,[15] because all '-isms' (the Hebrew prophets would have called them 'idols') will end in disillusionment.

In this short chapter, I have not been able to touch on these fascinating and important issues. Instead, I have concentrated on delineating the different natures of science and technology and their relationship in the modern world, and on discussing why technology necessarily entails risks. An appreciation of these basic issues provides a firm foundation for critical reflection on ethical, political and other questions raised by science and technology. The recently launched AS level 'Perspectives on Science' shows one way in which such material can be integrated into a coherent curriculum. When such integrated teaching and learning becomes widespread, science and technology citizenship education can be considered to have come of age.

Notes

1. Jim Crowther, Ian Martin and Mae Shaw (eds), *Renewing Democracy in Scotland* (Leicester: National Institute of Adult Continuing Education (England and Wales), 2003). Here and below, references are selected for their value as further reading.
2. Tom Conlon, 'The politics of technological change', in Crowther, Martin and Shaw, *Renewing Democracy in Scotland*, pp. 185–6.
3. For a philological history, see Carl Mitcham, *Thinking through Technology: The Path between Engineering and Philosophy* (Chicago and London: University of Chicago Press, 1994), ch. 5.
4. Amos Funkenstein, *Theology and the Scientific Imagination from the middle ages to the seventeenth century* (New Jersey: Princeton University Press, 1986), ch. V.
5. Mitcham, *Thinking through Technology*, p. 208.
6. For the ethical issues, see Donald Bruce and Ann Bruce (eds), *Engineering Genesis: The Ethics of Genetic Engineering in Non-Human Species* (London: Earthscan, 1999).
7. For a superb introduction to social complexity, see Philip Ball, *Critical Mass: how one thing leads to another* (London: Arrow Books, 2004).
8. Richard Wilson, 'Analysing the daily risks of life', in *Technology Review* 81, 1, pp. 41–6; reproduced in reference 14 below.
9. R. D. Clarke, *Journal of the Institute of Actuaries* 72 (1946), p. 481.
10. For an illuminating case study involving a communications mast, see A. T. Gavin and D. Catney, 'Addressing a community's

cancer cluster concerns', in *Ulster Medical Journal* 75, 3 (2006), pp. 195–9.

11. See John Ziman, *Reliable Knowledge: an exploration of the grounds for belief in science* (Cambridge: Cambridge University Press, 1978).
12. See John Ziman, *Prometheus Bound: science in a dynamic steady state* (Cambridge: Cambridge University Press, 1994), for a detailed introduction.
13. Henry N. Pollack, *Uncertain Science, Uncertain World* (Cambridge: Cambridge University Press: 2003) offers a readable account, with many examples taken from the climate change debate.
14. Bjørn Lomborg, *The Skeptical Environmentalist: Measuring the Real State of the World* (Cambridge: Cambridge University Press, 2001), chs 4 and 5.
15. Tzvetan Todorov, *Hope and Memory* (London: Atlantis Books, 2005) relates scientism to political totalitarianism.

Bioethics and Responsible Citizenship

Rodney S. Taylor

Rapid advances in the life sciences present a future full of promise and danger. Whether that future is more full of promise or danger is determined in part by what our societies decide to do with these advances. In democratic societies, this determination entails negotiations between interested parties, discussions about the nature of human life, and debates about right and wrong. The fruitfulness of these negotiations, discussions and debates depends in large part on the quality of citizens who are participating in them.

What is more, bioethics is not merely about policies, and citizenship is not just about how we contribute to policy formation. In reality, bioethics pervades our lives. Do we seek cosmetic surgery? Do we use IVF? Do we test our children for genetic disease? We need skills of deliberation to make these decisions, indeed to identify which decisions need to be made in the first place. Our decisions contribute to cultural habits that make some advances seem inevitable (now IVF seems a straightforward practice; thirty years ago, it was controversial). Only by 'growing' citizens capable of reflecting honestly about how they seek treatments – how they face life and death – will we have a real opportunity to seek the promises of advances in life sciences while avoiding the dangers.

In this article, I want to analyse how we are taught to talk about bioethical issues to shed light on the ways which we can better 'grow' citizens capable of thinking through these questions. I will begin with some background on the emergence of bioethics. I will then focus on the famous four principles – autonomy, justice, beneficence and non-maleficence – that form the heart of much bioethical discussion and education. After explaining how these principles are used, I will discuss the strengths and weaknesses of this principle-based approach. I hope to demonstrate why, whatever their uses, this approach is problematic if we want to 'grow' citizens. Having made the case for a different, more fluid approach to teaching and talking about bioethics, I will move on to explore that more open-ended approach in a discussion of what Christian theological perspectives may contribute to debates within bioethics.

Background

The intersection of medicine, biology and ethics is not a new topic. The Hippocratic Oath, which emerged sometime before the second century BC, indicates the long history of our concern about the ethics of biology and medicine.[1] What is new, however, is both the effectiveness, for good or ill, of our interventions into human biology and the way in which western societies, especially Anglo-Saxon ones, have decided to talk about these questions.

Although ethical issues related to medicine or biology stretch back into prehistory, the word 'bioethics' did not emerge until the early 1970s; nor did bioethics, as an academic discipline and as a way of thinking about ethical issues concerning biology or medicine. Today bioethics includes numerous professional organisations, degree programmes, textbooks, etc.

The rise of bioethics, however, does not make sense apart from three important developments. First is what Michel Foucault termed bio-power.[2] Briefly, with this term Foucault sought to explain a shift in attitudes toward political power. In the pre-modern world, the power of the sovereign was less to give life than to take it, hence the role of capital punishment as the prerogative of the monarch. The rise of the modern sciences and the shift to democratic humanism altered both the possibilities and understandings of political power. Now government has 'the function of administering life'[3]. By providing and/or regulating health care, education and the arts, political power is used to shape human life positively. With this move, however, the authority of government extends to most aspects of human life such that, perhaps ironically, modern governments have far more control over the details of human life than did the supposed autocrats of old. How does this relate to bioethics? If Foucault is right, it means that governments need codes of ethics and mechanisms of control to carry out better their expansive regulatory functions. Bioethics can serve 'as a broker of exotic biotechnologies' to the wider, sometimes sceptical, public,[4] thereby advancing government policy.

This need fits with a second trend in western life, noted by Max Weber: the emphasis upon a rational ordering of processes within complex bureaucratic societies. Weber set out three modes of authority: traditional, charismatic and rational-legal.[5] The third marks the dominant mode of authority in our era. In this mode, society is organised around technical, rational and seemingly neutral scientific principles that are beyond dispute. Formal rationality, which Weber contrasts with substantive rationality, is the means by which rational-legal authority seeks to provide a scientifically and rationally legitimate way of talking about issues.[6]

Formal rationality sets standards for reasoning without debating the ends or goods for which one reasons. So, for instance, we might set formal standards (say, student test scores) for determining whether education is successful or not, all the while ignoring deeper questions of what constitutes quality education and why we should want quality education in the first place (for job training? to make people well-rounded?). In contrast, substantive rationality leaves open these trickier questions about the goods for which we reason. If we want education to be more than job training, if we want it to cultivate more esoteric skills such as wisdom, then perhaps test scores and other supposedly objective measures may not be useful tools for determining whether education is successful.

The very appeal of formal rationality is that it ignores divisive questions such as the purpose of education (or biomedical intervention into human life). Rather, we can turn to these clearly articulated, (supposedly) rationally defensible principles or measurements that all 'clear-thinking' people will embrace.

The third important development was the emergence of eugenics in the nineteenth century. After Darwin shattered the idea that human nature was somehow static – after we learned to see what constituted a human as more malleable than we previously thought – some people began to wonder whether we might not be able to improve the human race through selective breeding, forced sterilisation of 'undesirables', etc. Darwin's cousin, Francis Galton, coined the term eugenics from the Greek meaning 'good birth'.[7] Although eugenics is often associated with Nazi ideology, in fact, for many it was considered a progressive, humanistic political stance until the Second World War.[8] Even after the War, dreams of genetic utopia died hard, and eugenics re-emerged in disguised form. Reactions against this genetic utopianism sparked debates in the United States that led directly to the emergence of bioethics as a means of regulating scientific practices.

The combination of these three trends encouraged the development of bioethics as a freestanding academic discipline. The complicated debates of the 1960s that pitted scientists, philosophers and theologians against one another gave way to a more manageable discussion centred on the universally accepted principles that bioethics provided.[9]

The Four Principles of Bioethics

By the early 1980s, the four principles of bioethics – autonomy, justice, beneficence and nonmaleficence – were firmly established through the publication of Tom Beauchamp's and James Childress's totemic *Principles of Biomedical Ethics*. These principles are 'fundamental precepts', that is, they are basic ethical commitments that should hold true in any society. Nonetheless, there may be exceptions in which the principles are not asserted absolutely.[10]

A brief rundown of the principles:

1. *Autonomy* – This principle emphasises the moral integrity of the patient or subject. From this principle derives the strong emphasis upon the consent of the patient or subject in bioethical discourse. If the 2004 Human Tissue Act in the United Kingdom is any indication, consent has become the *sine qua non* of bioethical discourse.
2. *Justice* – As Beauchamp and Childress describe it, justice in bioethics focuses on both the proper treatment of people (i.e. not treating people unequally) and on the proper distribution of medical, social and scientific benefits. Although justice may be one of the key political ideas of modern western societies, it actually plays a rather limited role in bioethics.

3. *Beneficence* – The focus here is upon doing good for others. Doing good is an active commitment to seeking the welfare of the other person.
4. *Nonmaleficence* – This principle encapsulates the classic *primum non nocere*, 'First, do no harm'. Unlike beneficence, nonmaleficence focuses on what is not done; hence it is a more limiting, passive principle.

The principles are intended to work together. So, for instance, doing good for others can become tyrannical, hence the need to respect autonomy. But respecting autonomy does not mean that we ignore the good that needs to be done. Rather, it means that we do not force that good upon people. Likewise, in and of itself, avoiding harm does not commit one to really engage with a patient or subject. But if you are going to treat her justly or do good for her, avoiding harm cannot be allowed to devolve into some minimalist ethic.

The strengths of this principle-based approach are obvious. These four principles (ideally) cut to the heart of the moral matter and allow those using them both to get a better grasp of what is really at stake in any given bioethical decision and to provide an indication of how to take decisions forward in a manner that honours proper ethical commitments to those principles. They also avoid confused debates by setting terms and standards that all participants can use. The principles are potentially broad enough to allow people from very different political, religious or ideological perspectives to use them without feeling the need to violate their core commitments.[11] In other words, this four-principle approach seems ideally suited to democratic societies.

Problems with the Principle Approach

However, the weaknesses, although less apparent, are real. Critiques of this kind of principle-based approach are extensive,[12] but I will focus briefly on three criticisms here. First, do these principles really get to the heart of the moral matter? Second, does the consensus these principles supposedly represent really overlap with the various groups that make up society (secularists, Christians, Muslims, libertarians, conservatives, etc.), or does it merely impose a way of talking about certain issues in biology and ethics upon these groups? Third, do these principle-based approaches really provide the tools needed to 'grow' citizens capable of exercising beneficial influence on our political and social lives?

Do the four principles rightly describe what is at stake morally? Is euthanasia just a matter of autonomy, justice, beneficence or nonmaleficence? How we describe acts determines in part how we judge them.[13] For instance, we realise that 'killing' is often an inadequate description of an act, so we develop terms such as murder, manslaughter and self defence to discriminate among various types of killing. Description, then, is a part of judgement. The four principles too often provide inadequate guidance on this kind of question, which means that the moral problem is under-described: we do not really know what we are talking about because we lack the tools needed to describe it adequately, much less, truthfully. The result is a form of moral deliberation that may satisfy the formal rationality of the four principles, but cannot really lead to discussions of the deeper human goods that make bioethical questions important in the first place.

Second, the claim in the overlapping consensus model is that shared principles can be derived from the 'thick', complex moral understandings that make up a given community's life.[14] So, for instance, the principle of autonomy could be seen as a secular analogy for the Christian and Jewish claim that humans are made in the image of God. Both views, it would be argued, reflect a moral demand that we respect others. While the principle of autonomy is clearly designed to foster a respect for an individual's self-determination, it is not clear that the theology behind the image of God claims in the Genesis account can fit such an understanding. Being made in the image of God could well imply that humans are not only to be respected, but that they were created to live in a certain fashion. So, where the principle of autonomy might support euthanasia – we should all determine our own fate – it is far less clear that traditional understandings of what it means to be made in the image of God would do so.

At best, the richness of the image of God metaphor is being watered down – 'thinned' out – to fit the principle of autonomy. Overlapping consensus does not exist, at least in this case. Rather, it's closer to colonisation, with the principle of autonomy subverting the image of God metaphor to its own ends. If taken too literally or narrowly, the danger is that by failing to take seriously the different cultural and social perspectives that people bring to their citizenship, the four-principles approach severs debate about bioethical questions from the things that actually matter in people's lives. The result is tepid discussions that often focus narrowly on rights to the exclusion of richer arguments.[15]

The third problem is whether such a principle-focused approach is the best way to grow citizens. Returning to Weber's point about formal rationality gives us an insight into this question. Formal rationality seeks to develop techniques for managing society. By thinking in terms of techniques, practitioners tend to reduce all problems to technical ones. There are trends in education where teachers and students are reduced to measurable outputs (say, exam results), that allow managers to demonstrate that their techniques are working, excluding all the arts and subtleties of good teaching and rich classroom experiences. The resulting measures may miss out on both the strengths *and* weaknesses of the actual teaching that is going on.

How does this translate to bioethics? By focusing discussion about bioethical questions so narrowly around the four principles, the richness and reality of what is actually at stake in these discussions may be lost. Students may demonstrate a facile ability to recount and deploy the four principles, but they will not necessarily have any grasp of what is being debated. Bioethical education becomes a technique designed to foster a very narrow outcome – learning the four principles – rather than a means of growing citizens who are able to contribute robustly to these complex discussions about biology, medicine and ethics. We can see this as an embrace of expertise – specialised technical knowledge – over against an appreciation of wisdom, of how to live well.

Our problem is that, as formulated around the four principles, bioethics may satisfy the technical, bureaucratic rationality of modern societies – it may provide a language which allows authorities to push forward scientific research in a manner that avoids too much politically destabilising debate about the controversial questions that emerge in these areas – but it does not really accomplish the democratic function of shaping citizens capable of contributing to these debates. In effect, this 'technicist'[16] approach leads to stunted growth.

The four-principle approach, if taken too literally would tend to exclude richer perspectives because they do not meet the technical criteria (autonomy, justice, beneficence and nonmaleficence) for participating in the debate. Insights derived from descriptions that did not fit these categories would be deemed inessential or perhaps even inadmissible. As a result, moral conversation is seriously restricted, and acts are inadequately defined. Far from getting to the heart of the matter, the four-principle approach can delude us into thinking we have a grasp of the problems at hand when we have no real idea what we are talking about or what is at stake morally.

Toward a More Substantive Approach

Behind these problems lurks a complex question of how humans 'grow' morally. I need to make a few points to support the claims I am going to make. First, the 'technical' approach to education cannot capture the actual richness of human learning. Humans are not machines into which we simply insert data, but are beings that learn through exploration, failure, imagination, touching, seeing, feeling, memorising, thinking, etc. Merely repeating four principles mantra-like may construct citizens capable of narrowly applying four principles, but it will not grow ones capable of exercising their full moral and intellectual skills in exploring how the life sciences can enhance or threaten our lives.

Second, there is no neutral position (whether conceived as a starting place from which all rational people may work out their beliefs or a realm where certain claims – especially complex ones such as the nature of human life – are beyond dispute) around which to develop the curriculum. The 'overlapping consensus' model may not pretend there is no neutral starting place, but it does assume that we can somehow leave behind our traditions, beliefs, etc. in order to fashion a neutral realm – the realm of formal rationality – to discuss bioethical questions. By failing to recognise how we bring to our deliberations the complex narratives and descriptions that make up our moral communities (churches, mosques, circles of friends, political parties), the four-principle approach deprives us of the rich perspectives, knowledges and understandings that are drawn from those communities and ignores the moral growth that has already taken place before we began the formal process of learning bioethics. These 'traditioned' ways of thinking[17] make up the actual content of the societies in which we live. The question is whether we will take seriously how those traditions can enrich our collective moral lives.

Finally, we cannot live compartmentalised lives, being a public citizen here and private person there. Focusing teaching solely or even primarily through the four principles creates a situation in which either our commitments (to the four principles on one hand and to the richer understandings of our 'traditioned' moral communities on the other) are in conflict or one set of commitments is subsumed into the other.

Keeping these points in mind, we can move forward to see how Christian theological perspectives (or perspectives from other 'traditioned' ways of thinking) may contribute to the way we talk about, hence learn about, bioethics. To do so will move us from a formal rationality to a substantive one, which will better connect the discrete issues of bioethics to the larger fabric of the good life.

Christian Contributions to Bioethics

If the four principles are not a useful starting point for bioethical reflection, where could we start? Why not ask, first, what it means to be human.[18] The reason bioethics is important to us – the reason why we want to discuss whether genetic testing is a good idea or whether organ transplantation is good practice – is because these things either enhance or hamper our humanity. But to know whether something is enhancement or harm, we have to have an idea about what it means to be human. Of course, the answer to that question is hardly uncontroversial. The precise reason bioethical language was invented was to get around the seemingly endless disagreements about these kinds of fundamental philosophical and theological questions. Yet, as irresolvable as these questions may seem (and be), we simply have no other place to start thinking about bioethical questions if we want to encourage people to think seriously – substantively in Weber's terminology – about these matters.

From a Christian perspective, we can start, as mentioned above, with the claim that humans are created in the image of God. Even within Christianity, understandings of that claim are contested. Being made in the image of God has been linked with everything from rationality to our relational nature. However we might describe it precisely, the claim does indicate that there is a 'givenness' to human nature. To say that humans are made in the image of God is to claim that there is something about them that is not merely subject to the biological and psychological changes humans undergo through history.

What might this claim mean for bioethics? Think about so-called 'designer' babies. What might the four principles say? It could be seen as a violation of the autonomy of the unborn, but that's a controversial claim as autonomy is not normally granted to the unborn for the simple reason that they are not autonomous. Before birth, children are completely dependent upon their mothers. What about justice? If we are improving peoples' lives, helping them overcome genetic 'disabilities' or 'weaknesses', how is that unjust? If justice has anything to say, it may say that we should require parents to make use of the best available techniques of genetic manipulation to ensure a good life for their offspring. Beneficence and nonmaleficence are the most applicable principles, but as long as we are 'improving' people, what harm is being done?

By themselves, the four principles raise no serious questions against 'designer' babies. What about being made in the image of God? Here we have a richer tool for thinking about the question of whether or not we should attempt to produce humans in this manner. For by toying with our genetic code, we are potentially changing our nature. By discussing what that claim means, we get into a deeper discussion about what it means to be human and what it might mean to alter our genetic make-up. Those deeper discussions allow us to genuinely 'grow' morally by helping us to see things differently and to understand better what is at stake.

For instance how do we describe the bearing of children? Is it procreation or reproduction?[19] 'Reproduction' fits well with an industrial, technical mindset, the kind of mindset that also welcomes positive genetic manipulation as progress. In contrast, 'procreation' implicitly refers not just to creation, but to creator. By describing the having of babies in one way rather than another we have shifted the focus of discussion to one in which we are questioning the fundamental shape of human life, rather than just limiting ourselves to four principles.

If the generation of life is procreation, then we are turned to the one who creates and the gift of creation that is given. While western thinkers and western mores tend to emphasise gift-giving as a one-way process – if something is truly a gift, no strings will be attached – anthropological literature abounds with examples of how in most societies gift and giver cannot be so easily separated.[20] In reality, gifts are extensions of givers; gifts are ways to embody social relationships.

Receiving gifts, then, binds us into a relationship with the giver. Social conventions allow us some leeway in how we receive gifts, but not absolute freedom. We may exchange a book that someone has given us for another book or similar gift, but to use it to kindle a fire would not be acceptable. Burning the book would insult the giver. In other words, what we do with a gift speaks to the quality of our reception of it. How, then, should we receive the gift of our lives and the lives of our children? Do 'design' and 'control' fit with procreation? By extensively trying to manipulate procreation we may find ourselves turning it into something it was not intended to be, turning a book into kindling.[21]

If gifts restrict or obligate us, can they not be dangerous? Should we not fear the 'tyranny of the gift'?[22] However, what if the giver is one we need not fear? Such would be the Christian claim, that the God who gave God's only Son to redeem the world is a God who can be trusted to give good gifts, gifts that do not tyrannise. These claims bind reality and our lives into a certain kind of relationship, helping us to see life and the world as gifts to accept rather than problems to be overcome through genetic manipulation.

Reasoning through claims such as these, as opposed to restricting debate to the four principles, leads to a much more substantive description of human life, and raises serious concerns about such genetic manipulation that the four principles would paper over. Of course, my claim is a more controversial one, for if one does not accept the reality of this God, then the claims I have built on that God's nature become problematic. Should we not, then, turn to the four principles after all? No, because the one who rejects my God may have her own substantive account of human life to provide. In talking about these rich conceptions of life we can gain a deeper understanding of both the importance of human life and the seriousness entailed in altering it. We may not agree so readily on what to do, but working through the richer descriptions can foster a deeper understanding of the moral life in regard to genetic manipulation in ways that grow us morally and make us more vibrant participants in public debates, which, in turn, can lead to more morally serious policies and practices.

Theology can also help re-situate other debates. Consider euthanasia. Normally, euthanasia is argued about in terms of human dignity. Either human dignity is honoured by recognising autonomy and allowing patients to choose the manner of their own death, or it is dishonoured by supposing that killing an innocent person is ever justified. The four principles provide muddled guidance. Autonomy clearly favours patient prerogative. Justice is uncertainly applied. Either justice is done in giving the one who wishes to die her due by allowing her to die a dignified death, or it is violated by killing an innocent person. How you choose to assign justice here depends in large part on whether, *before deliberation*, you think euthanasia is a good idea. In other words, in this case the principle of justice, far from actively shaping deliberation, will more likely just facilely confirm the opinion one already has.

Beneficence and nonmaleficence fall into the same difficulty in this debate. Whether one is doing good or harm is not objectively determined, but rather depends on presupposed notions of good and harm. If allowing someone to linger beyond what seems a dignified point seems cruel, then euthanasia is doing good and avoiding harm. If it is nothing but murder by another name, then it is doing harm and rejecting good. Once again, the four principles are less than helpful. Far from aiding deliberation, they may deceive you into thinking you have reflected on the problem when in reality you have just fitted the principles to the outcome you wished to get to in the first place. And for those genuinely conflicted? Because justice, beneficence and nonmaleficence are such vague categories, the principles really do not help.

How might theology clarify? Consider Michael Banner's comparison of martyrdom and euthanasia.[23] In this age of the suicide bomber, we are apt to think of martyrs as those who court death and kill others in the process. But there are alternative forms of martyrdom, notably the one practised by early Christians. Here the martyr does not seek death, nor does she kill others in the process; rather, she does not resist the death others would impose upon her for her refusal to do what they wish (normally honouring Caesar as a god). As Banner argues, her stance is not an acceptance of death, but a 'dying which is filled with hope',[24] specifically hope in the resurrection and everlasting life. In contrast, euthanasia embraces death. Faced with the inevitability of death, the sick person, like the fox who could not get the grapes, says, 'I don't want to live anyway'.

Euthanasia seems like a rational, merciful response in large part because it responds to two other problematic attitudes toward death: neglect and overtreatment.[25] Faced with the inevitability of the death, doctors are tempted to neglect the patient (there is nothing else they can do, so they benignly withdraw) or to superhuman efforts to deny the inescapable reality (undertaking measures that extend life marginally while creating the indignity that makes euthanasia seem merciful). Banner notes the dilemma is a false one. For instance, hospices represent an alternative form of dying that neither denies nor embraces the reality of death. At root, then, is a misunderstanding of the place of and fear of death. To that misunderstanding and fear, Christian theology counterpoints the hope of the martyr, who does not avoid death at all costs, but neither seeks a false glory in dying as a martyr.

The pains of death are real, both on those dying and those left behind. Christian theology has no interest in denying that reality. What it does deny (along with many different theologies, albeit with a very different focus) is any claim that death is the final word on the creature. Life defines the creature – God 'is not God of the dead but of the living' (Mark 12:27). But euthanasia turns from life. It rejects the possibility of good in a life that, on its own, would continue.

In contrast to the four principles, a discussion of classic Christian understandings of martyrdom digs deeper into what is at stake morally in euthanasia. Euthanasia cannot be reduced to a matter of individual autonomy (as a four-principles approach tends to do), but is a reflection of our wider understanding of the value and purpose of human life. To allow euthanasia to be discussed solely in terms of autonomy ignores how the practice of euthanasia contributes to what Pope John Paul II called the culture of death, a culture in which the value of human life is lessened. Such lessening is not easily contained to one field, but can become a habit of thinking and action that demeans and trivialises life.

Conclusion

Life has a richness that four principles cannot capture. The substantive rationality of theologies and philosophies is an important tool to help us remain grounded in our humanity. Classrooms that discuss the kinds of questions posed by theologies and philosophies rather than having students memorise four principles will give children the opportunity to explore more deeply what their humanity means for them and their society. Such children will be better prepared to be the kinds of citizens society needs if it is going to have any hope of discerning what constitutes harm and benefit as the life sciences continue to challenge our understanding of what being human means.

As I hope is apparent, the real problem is not merely whether we use the four principles to discuss these questions, but whether we can escape the constricting binds of a formal rationality that corrupts our moral deliberation and growth. Fruitful deliberation depends upon people who have the character and knowledge necessary to explore how novel problems relate to their ongoing struggle to be truly human, to live abundantly, as Jesus might have said (John 10:10).[26]

Notes

1. For a brief summary of medical ethics before bioethics see Albert R. Jonsen, *The Birth of Bioethics* (Oxford: Oxford University Press, 1998), pp. 3–27.
2. What follows is merely a brief recapitulation of Foucault's argument. See *The History of Sexuality*, vol. 1, trans. Robert Hurley (London: Penguin Books, 1978), pp. 135–59 for a fuller treatment.

3. Foucault, p. 138.
4. M. L. Tina Stevens, *Bioethics in America* (Baltimore: Johns Hopkins University Press, 2000), p. 153.
5. Max Weber, *Economy and Society*, vol. 1, ed. Guenther Roth and Claus Wittich (New York: Bedminster Press, 1968), pp. 215–16. Weber explores these three in detail on pp. 217–54.
6. Weber, pp. 25–6. John Evans takes this point from Weber to advance his own critique of bioethics, to which I am in debt, in *Playing God: Human Genetic Engineering and the Rationalization of Public Bioethical Debate* (London: University of Chicago Press, 2002).
7. Evans, *Playing God*, p. 47.
8. Ibid., p. 48.
9. For contrasting views of whether this development can be seen as a good or bad thing, see Jonsen (for whom it is primarily a good thing) and Evans (who disagrees).
10. Tom L. Beauchamp and James F. Childress, *Principles of Biomedical Ethics* (5th edn; Oxford: Oxford University Press, 2001), pp. 4–5.
11. This 'overlapping consensus', as John Rawls terms it, will be discussed below.
12. For instance, Stanley Hauerwas, *The Peaceable Kingdom: A Primer for Christian Ethics* (Notre Dame: University of Notre Dame Press, 1983), pp. 19–22.
13. Charles Pinches, *Theology and Action: After Theory in Christian Ethics* (Grand Rapids: William B. Eerdmans, 2002), pp. 115–16.
14. The political philosopher John Rawls is the central figure in the development of the overlapping consensus model. See his *Political Liberalism* (rev. edn; New York: Columbia University Press, 1996), pp. 133–72.
15. Stevens's book makes this kind of argument in relation to the right-to-die movement and how professional bioethics actually obscured the moral issues at stake by not being better embedded in the diverse social and cultural realities of the United States.
16. Stevens, p. 468, footnote 20.
17. Alasdair MacIntyre, *After Virtue* (2nd edn; Notre Dame: University of Notre Dame Press, 1985), pp. 221–2. For a fuller treatment of this mode of thinking and a contrast of it with other modes of thinking, see MacIntyre's *Three Rival Versions of Moral Enquiry* (London: Duckworth, 1990).

18. Focusing on our humanity in this manner may create theological problems. See Amy Laura Hall, 'Finding the Human in Christian Bioethics', http://www.cbhd.org/resources/bioethics/hall_2006-04-07.htm (accessed 19 February 2008). I hope it is clear that the turn to the human must also be a turn to the God Christians proclaim.
19. Gilbert Meilaender, *Bioethics: A Primer for Christians* (2nd edn; Grand Rapids: William B. Eerdmans, 2005), p. 11.
20. Marcel Mauss's classic, early twentieth-century study *The Gift: Forms and Functions of Exchange in Archaic Societies* (trans. Ian Cunnison; London: Routledge & Kegan Paul, 1969), opened a fruitful avenue for analysis and speculation that still shapes social science research and philosophical/theological argumentation.
21. For another, different theological critique of genetic manipulation see Gilbert Meilaender, 'Designing Our Descendents', *First Things* 109 (January 2001), pp. 25–8.
22. Renee C. Fox and Judith P. Swazey use this phrase in their studies of organ donation and transplantation practices. The term describes the fear medical professionals have that the shadow of the donor shall hover unceasingly over the recipient of a transplanted organ. See *Spare Parts: Organ Replacement in American Society* (Oxford: Oxford University Press, 1992), pp. 39–42.
23. Michael Banner, *Christian Ethics and Contemporary Moral Problems* (Cambridge: Cambridge University Press, 1999), pp. 68–83.
24. Ibid., p. 83.
25. Ibid., pp. 75–7.
26. I am grateful to my colleague, Almut Caspary, for her careful reading and insightful comments of an earlier draft of this paper.

Environmental Citizenship – Agents for Environmental Justice

Eurig Scandrett

> environmental awareness … environmental literacy … environmental responsibility … environmental competence … might be regarded as the marks of a good environmental citizenship.

> Being a 'citizen' is … more than being a subject, or a client, or even a customer. It implies active engagement on our part … and it requires that our engagement is bolstered by defined rights and that we are given access to detailed information about what is being done in our name.

Knowledge of the extent of environmental destruction sets a challenge to our understanding of our responsibilities as citizens. The quotations above demonstrate a tension which reflects the contested political implications of citizenship. In the first, the citizen is on good behaviour while 'others' keep the place in order – by implication, a bad citizen is one who damages the environment through ignorance or irresponsibility. The citizen in the second quotation participates in changing things – the 'others' can't be trusted to keep the place in order. Active participation by citizens is required to prevent the actions of those who have the power and tendency to damage the environment. The first, passive citizen was being advocated by Michael Forsyth,

Conservative Secretary of State for Scotland, in his preface to the report of his working group on environmental education: *Learning for Life* (1993).[1] The second citizen was the aspiration of Kevin Dunion, as Chief Executive of Friends of the Earth Scotland, in his introduction to the publication *Protecting our Environment* (1997).[2]

Not only the quality of our responsibility to the environment, but the membership of the citizenly community is contested in the idea of environmental citizenship.

That we are citizens, not just of a state or society but of the earth with all its interconnected ecological relations, is increasingly being advocated. Membership of the citizenship community can no longer be assumed to be restricted to compatriots, or even to humanity, or to the living: arguably we have citizenship responsibilities to global humanity, to animals and plants, mountains and forests, future generations.

Reflecting on the implications for environmental citizenship can take us in different directions. Writers such as Peter Christoff and Mike Mills, for example, seek to extend the moral community with which citizenship representation and responsibility is shared, to global humanity, non-human ecology and future generations (in Doherty and de Geus 1996).[3] Others, such as Andrew Dobson (2003),[4] while not engaging with speculative cosmology, present a form of environmental citizenship based on relations of social justice.

Dobson develops a conception of post-cosmopolitan citizenship, in which globalisation and ecological destruction demand a citizenship which goes beyond the territorial nation state. However, globalisation is unequal and unjust, and therefore requires an asymmetrical citizenship in which rights and responsibilities are determined by *relations of actual harm* conducted through the global economy. The structure of the global economy is such that to conduct normal everyday life in the UK (as in Western Europe and

North America) a citizen inflicts actual harm on citizens elsewhere in the world. These relations of actual harm between global citizens mean that citizens in the global North have a disproportionate responsibility and those in the South, disproportionately have rights.

Moreover, Dobson argues, those rights, and especially these responsibilities, are citizenly, not moral. Moral actions, while they may be highly virtuous, are freely chosen and may therefore be freely withdrawn. A citizenship action by contrast is material: it emerges from the condition of being embedded in a relation of actual harm. Action for global and environmental justice is therefore a civic responsibility or a civil right. Reducing our use of fossil fuels, buying fairly traded goods, challenging the expansion of supermarket hegemony, these must be cast not as moral actions but citizenly responsibilities. Acting for justice is the work of a citizen. By insisting on a material, rather than a moral conception of justice, Dobson's view is distinguished from those debates around ecological citizenship which focus on extending the moral community to include non-human nature and future generations.

The advantage of conceptualising actions as citizenly rather than moral is that they become a normal part of everyday conduct, not an item of choice for the especially good. Environmental responsibility can therefore, according to Dobson, safely be taught to children in schools' citizenship education without infringing the ideal of impartiality and neutrality in liberal education.

Ironically, Dobson uses as his model for moral (as distinct from citizenly) action the parable of the 'Good Samaritan', which in gospel terms is set in the context of a debate about love of neighbour and the 'outsider' (Luke 10:25–37). However, our character is more significant for being a Samaritan than for being good and it could be argued that the parable's question 'which of these three … made himself a neighbour to the man who fell into the hands of robbers?' could equally be applied today, with 'citizen' replacing 'neighbour'. To replay the injunction to 'love the lord your God with all your heart and all your soul and your fellow citizen as yourself' would beg the question 'who is my fellow citizen?' This question would surely be answered, with Dobson, 'My fellow citizen is one to whom I am connected because my actions cause her/him actual harm'. The Good Samaritan may be a more appropriate model for the good citizen than for the moral actor.

Despite his choice of metaphor, two areas of Dobson's thesis will be used as a point of departure for the argument developed here. The first is the relations of actual harm, which are enacted not just through globalised inequality, but in the social structures through which the inequality is ordered. The second is his application through the citizenship curriculum in schools, which is perhaps more appropriately conducted through popular education. Finally, an example of the use of popular education by Friends of the Earth Scotland and Queen Margaret University is described.

Dobson is surely right to situate citizenship action in the context of injustices which result from the relations of global production and consumption. However, this analysis should account for the complexities of global inequalities in terms of class in particular. The inequalities of globalisation are not entirely between 'developed' and 'developing' countries. Inequalities in the form of late capitalism in which we live, continue to be class-based, which increasingly take on global dimensions. Sklair (2001),[5] for example, identifies the emergence of a transnational capitalist class, whose origins and residence are in diverse countries but whose interests and culture are common and increasingly non-territorial.

The polarity of injustice is more complex than North–South, but cannot be adequately explained by class relations. A rich member of the transnational capitalist class who is also a citizen of India, living in Kolkata, will presumably have the same post-cosmopolitan citizenship responsibilities as a similar citizen of the UK living in Edinburgh. Moreover, what are we to make of the citizenly responsibilities of a poor working-class British citizen living in substandard public housing, whose daily business involves reproducing a relation of actual harm to people in the global South (by using fossil fuel-generated electricity to keep warm in a poorly insulated building), but who is thus also a victim of actual harm? Dobson's analysis allows us to discuss the complexity of rights and responsibilities which citizens should claim or exercise, on the basis of their position in global relations of production and consumption.

These relations are of course dominated by capitalist economics. The relations of actual harm in capitalist economy, especially those of an environmental nature, may be principally categorised as having two forms. One is the externalisation of costs and the other is the devaluation of resources. The externalisation of costs is the mechanism whereby economic activities ignore the damage caused to society or to the environment because the value of this damage is not recognised by the price system. The cost to the environment appears, off balance sheet, as a by-product of the production process – in Michael Jacob's memorable metaphor, the invisible elbow which is connected to Adam Smith's invisible hand (Jacobs 1992).[6] In fact, as Joan Martinez-Alier (2002)[7] has pointed out, externalisation is not an accidental by-product of the capitalist production system but an active attempt to offload costs in a competitive environment.

Marx identified how the creative productivity of the worker is devalued in capitalism. However, the value of natural resources is also systematically depressed in order for them to be used as commodity by capital. Indeed, the price which is allocated through the relations of supply and demand is a crude measure of the value of nature. Such valuation ignores the value of social and environmental resources to the people whose health, material conditions, aesthetic or spirituality is dependent on them, not to mention the intrinsic value which can be ascribed to these resources. Martinez-Alier (2002) draws attention to the conflicts of valuation which lead to social movements throughout the world, especially among people whose poverty gives them little purchase in the supply–demand equation. This 'environmentalism of the poor' is described by Martinez-Alier as a distinct stream of environmental movement which has resisted the devaluing of their environments.

Theologically, these movements may be recognised as among the poor who are blessed, to whom God is biased and in whom God acts in history. Environmental oppression is a mechanism of injustice, and the social movements who resist have an 'epistemological advantage' which challenges our valuation of the environment. Any understanding of environmental citizenship must take place alongside and in dialogue with these movements for environmental justice who are resisting the economic relations which tie us together in inflicting actual harm.

The second comment on Dobson is his proposal that, having identified a robust version of post-cosmopolitan environmental citizenship, he therefore wishes to use citizenship education as a mechanism for encouraging such citizenly behaviour among children. As various educational theorists have identified, the selection of a curriculum for schools has a function of reproducing relations of production and consumption in society. For example, Michael Apple (1990)[8] has explored the reproduction of hegemonic class relations through a political economy of knowledge and culture in schools. While this reproductive function is not exact, and opportunities exist for teachers to subvert or pupils to resist the curriculum, and for theorists like Dobson to develop more appropriate curricula, none the less, the curriculum remains essentially a selection from existing culture and knowledge, disconnected from the material conditions of the learner. Dobson's materialist understanding of citizenship deserves a materialist pedagogy. While there is undoubted value in introducing environmental citizenship into the school curriculum, its influence is likely to be limited. A potentially more powerful education for environmental citizenship would derive the curriculum from the actual lived experience of environmental harm and struggles for justice.

Materialist curricula and pedagogies have been developed particularly in the radical tradition of adult education. Ettore Gelpi's conception of lifelong education focuses on the experience of adults in relation to the struggle for dignity and rights. Adults, through their experience of work, unemployment, parenthood, migration, bureaucracy, etc. seek knowledge which is in their material interests. It is thus in the areas of social conflict that Gelpi sources the most fertile origins of a liberating curriculum for lifelong education: 'an idea of intrinsic adult learning situations whose knowledge-content is much more a function of the social relations of production than of the curriculum categories of schooling' (Griffin 1983).[9]

Paulo Freire (1972), in his *Pedagogy of the Oppressed*, developed a dialogical learning methodology in which the material situation of the oppressed becomes the origins of education, and enters into dialogue with the skills and knowledge of the teacher.[10] Freire applies this pedagogy in the context of liberation struggle and expects the teacher to be overtly politically committed. However, he challenges revolutionary leaders who apply the same 'banking' method of education as the oppressors, thereby denying the agency of the oppressed to bring their own experience and material conditions to the pedagogical relationship.

Freire's thinking was inspired as much by his theology as by Marxism and, following exile from his native Brazil, he was employed in the World Council of Churches. His pedagogical methodology has close parallels with that of Gustavo Guttierez and other theologians of liberation. Freirean methodology has been used by popular movements in Latin America and adapted for use in support of social and political change throughout the world (e.g. Kane 2001).[11] The Agents for Environmental Justice project at Friends of the Earth Scotland draws on Freirean methodology in support of community activists – environmental citizens – engaged in struggles for environmental justice in Scotland.

The demands of environmental citizenship therefore require an engagement with environmental justice – a struggle in dialogue with social movements who challenge the externalising of costs and devaluing of resources through the expression of alternative environmental value. Moreover, such dialogue is always to some extent educational: the responsibility for achieving justice requires a mutual learning between those who claim their rights when suffering actual harm, and those who inflict such harm. Such an educational dialogue has a place – alongside other forms of political struggle – in overturning the relations of actual harm produced by capitalism's requirement to devalue resources and externalise costs, and in developing an alternative valuation of humanity and our environment.

Friends of the Earth's work for environmental justice seeks to combine the experience of local struggles for a decent environment and those who act in solidarity with them, with the more global campaigns over resource consumption. Throughout the world, the finite resources are disproportionately used by the richest peoples and in rich countries such as Scotland. Therefore, environmental justice is described by the strap line: 'no less than a decent environment for all, with no more than our fair share of the earth's resources'.

The Agents for Environmental Justice project was conducted by Friends of the Earth Scotland in collaboration with Queen Margaret University, over three years from 2001–04. Funded by the Community Fund, it centred on providing relevant education to communities active in struggles for environmental justice. Twelve activists in different parts of Scotland were supported through a course of study in their communities and through residential teaching weekends located near to these communities. The student/activists are known as 'agents' because they act as community agents, mobilising and working with their communities rather than studying for personal certification alone.

The course used Freirean methodology to provide analytical knowledge and campaigning and community development skills, and also to respond with a curriculum relevant to the agents' local context. Political practice was given equal status with theoretical analysis, and the validation by Queen Margaret University as a Higher Education Certificate added value to the experience of the local activists. The curriculum was constantly negotiated between tutors and agents and assessments were designed to be useful in their campaigns. The twelve agents completed the course and were awarded a Higher Education Certificate in Environmental Justice in 2003.

The course has since been adapted for use through distance learning, making it affordable without significant grants and more accessible to a wider range of people, and is being offered as part of QMU's undergraduate and Continuing Professional Development programmes.

The experiences and contexts of the first group of agents is published as 'Voices from the Grassroots' in Friends of the Earth's handbook series *Redressing the Balance: working towards environmental justice in Scotland* (available from FoE Scotland or as pdf on http://www.foe-scotland.org.uk/nation/agents_handbooks.html). Here are a few examples of the activists who have benefited from the education, and the contexts in which they have used it.

Ann Coleman lives in the North Lanarkshire village of Greengairs, a community blighted by opencast coal mines and landfill sites on all sides. The community is an example of a 'sacrificial zone', in which one environmentally damaging activity follows another, and the planning process does little to prevent this. Ann's community has however become active in attempting to use the planning system and campaigning tools more effectively to try to prevent further damage, and to minimise the damage which has already occurred. They have developed a relationship with the landfill operators in order to demand the best standards of operation and to prevent toxic, unlicensed or unpleasant waste coming to the site. Ann has also taken her campaigns to the national level and lobbied to improve standards of waste management for other communities.

Aaron Forsyth is a crofter in the village of Scoraig in Wester Ross, situated on a peninsula between Loch Broom and Little Loch Broom. The community is highly dependent on these clean sea lochs for seaweed for fertilising organic crops and herbs for use and sale, for fishing and for tourism. Recent developments of salmon farms in the lochs are regarded by some as a threat to the unpolluted waters and therefore the livelihood and quality of life of the community. Salmon farms usually consist of densely stocked containers of live salmon immersed in coastal waters. Waste from surplus feed and excreta can concentrate in the lochs and damage the ecosystems. Fish are susceptible to diseases such as lice and this can spread into the wild salmon stocks. Chemical pesticides are added, which can then contaminate both water and fish meat. The limited employment which salmon farming brings must be seen against the damage to livelihoods of crofters and the fact that most salmon farms are owned by multinational corporations whose profits are not locally invested. Aaron and his community are campaigning to protect the marine environment, not only around their own township but throughout the north-west of Scotland where communities face a similar threat.

Nahid Aslam is active in her local Community Council in Edinburgh, seeking to improve the physical environment of her neighbourhood. She also has an interest in the environmental involvement of minority ethnic communities in Scotland, and in particular her own Punjabi community. Nahid notes how the exodus of many Punjabis from rural India and Pakistan was encouraged by the 'green revolution', which replaced traditional organic agriculture with high-yield, high-input varieties of crops, resulting in the displacement of small farmers by bigger landlords with access to capital. This process is likely to be repeated if genetically modified crops are introduced. Some of those who migrated to Scotland became an important source of resources for families and neighbours who remained.

Environmental justice became a major social force in the USA when minority ethnic communities mobilised against the dumping of toxic wastes in their neighbourhoods. Environmental racism in Scotland may take a different form, but it is still part of the experience of many black Scots and migrants in this country and those affected by this country throughout the world. Amadu Khan, an agent who works in Wester Hailes, has identified ways in which refugees fleeing social, environmental and economic conflicts are too often housed in the worst environments in Scotland and their participation in environmental improvements is often overlooked.

Poor quality and badly maintained public sector housing is an environmental injustice of neglect affecting many of Scotland's communities. Fuel poverty affects those who can hardly afford to heat their homes and at the same time wastes energy and contributes to climate change. Kirsten Marshall has been campaigning to improve housing conditions for her and her two daughters in Dundyvan in Coatbridge. Her experience is that the wealthier parts of the town have higher priorities for development, and even those amenities in her community are increasingly being taken over by those from outside who can afford to pay.

Joan Higginson has participated in community activities in Midlothian for years but her involvement in opposing the A701 Penicuik to Edinburgh road exposed her to environmental injustices in development planning. The road was proposed to go through several small towns which have suffered high unemployment with the closures of the deep mines, and also cut through several areas of nature conservation value in the Edinburgh greenbelt. In her experience, the granting of permission for the road had more to do with the economic development aspirations of the local authority, and political structures seemed to serve to exclude rather than involve the local communities in the decisions. She has undertaken local audits in the communities to assess what their sustainability needs are, and has also turned her attention to fighting the biotechnology and other developments which are attaching themselves to the unfinished road without adding to the economic wellbeing of the area.

The Agents for Environmental Justice project demonstrates the opportunities of education for citizenship when the resources for learning are matched to the communities who are engaged in struggles for justice. Such education is challenging for educators and educational institutions. But this project shows how a partnership between an environmental organisation committed to justice, and a higher education institution committed to widening participation, can achieve learning which is both academically rigorous and politically engaged.

Notes

1. *Learning for Life: a national strategy for environmental education in Scotland* (Edinburgh: The Scottish Office, 1993).
2. *Protecting our Environment: a citizen's guide to campaigning and environmental rights* (Edinburgh: Friends of the Earth Scotland, 1997).
3. B. Doherty and M. de Geus (eds), *Democracy and Green Political Thought: Sustainability, Rights and Citizenship* (London: Routledge, 1996).
4. A. Dobson, *Citizenship and the Environment* (Oxford: Oxford University Press, 2003).
5. L. Sklair, *The Transnational Capitalist Class* (Oxford: Blackwell, 2001).
6. M. Jacobs, *The Green Economy* (London: Pluto Press, 1992).
7. J. Martinez-Alier, *The Environmentalism of the Poor* (Cheltenham: Edward Elgar, 2002).
8. M. Apple, *Ideology and Curriculum* (New York: Routledge, 1990).
9. C. Griffin, *Curriculum Theory in Adult and Lifelong Education* (London: Croom Helm, 1983).
10. P. Freire, *Pedagogy of the Oppressed* (Harmondsworth: Penguin, 1972).
11. L. Kane, *Popular Education and Social Change in Latin America* (London: Latin America Bureau, 2001).

Citizenship, Culture and the Arts

Donald Smith

Introduction

At first glance Citizenship and the Arts seem to sit comfortably together, ready to trip neatly off the tongues of educators and curriculum designers. In reality, this juxtaposition goes straight to the heart of some acute dilemmas in contemporary arts provision, planning and funding.

If art of all kinds represents the free expression of creativity, albeit in social forms and contexts, then the idea of advancing 'citizenship values' as a cultural objective may seem contradictory or even threatening to artists. What about the awkward squads?

Of course, advocates of citizenship values are not so dumb, and clearly creative freedoms have an important place in a society which encourages individual rights and freedoms. However, such advocates need also to recognise that support for the arts and the application of such support in specific contexts has its own histories. Respect for democratic or artistic freedoms cannot be presumed even among educators.

Both the performing and the plastic arts were subject very early in human cultural development to the powers of patrons. Herein also lies a longstanding and troublesome distinction between 'high' and 'low' or popular culture. In general, such distinctions have little grounding in aesthetic analysis but much more relationship to the question of 'who pays?' If an art form such as folk song can be practised without the patronage of an economic elite, then it tends to be classified as popular art. By contrast, an art form which requires a patron's financial support because of its complexity or production requirements has often claimed the status of high art.

These distinctions were transferred to modern industrial societies – 'popular' becoming associated with the mass-produced or that financed by market demand, and 'high' with those arts requiring financial support before or beyond their income-earning capacity. Patrons dispensed support in line with a variety of aesthetic, social, political and economic motivations.

The patronage mentality passed over into the motivations and behaviour of government as well as economic elites. When, during the Second World War, the British government established a Committee for the Encouragement of Music and the Arts (CEMA), it was specifically to raise morale while implicitly encouraging support for a British way of life that encompassed enjoyment and *soi-disant* cultural freedoms.

In the postwar period these motivations transmuted into the idea that the arts were in themselves beneficial to the tone of the nation, contributing to an agenda of social and educational improvement. Maynard Keynes in particular was influential in the thinking of the postwar Labour government which resulted in the formation of the Arts Council of Great Britain in 1946, a direct successor to the wartime committee.

In Arts Council thinking from the start, the arts (for which read 'high arts') required financial subsidy in order that they could be given or taken to the population. Audiences would then receive the uplift of artistic experience and be individually and collectively improved. The language of patronage was quite explicit and the Arts Council report for 1952–3 strikes a characteristic note:

> The principle of collective patronage, like many other principles of British behaviour, has become accepted in a piecemeal, almost absent-minded fashion. There have been milestones, of course, in its development, such as the creation of The Arts Council, by Royal Charter, in 1946 and the inclusion in the Local Government Act of 1948 a brief, but significant, clause empowering local authorities to devote up to a 6^{d} rate (4½^{d} in Scotland) on entertainment and the arts.[1]

Like CEMA, the Arts Council formed a Scottish Committee and allocated Scotland a proportionate budget, though until 1952 the Edinburgh International Festival received its grant directly from London.

A Scottish Narrative

For the purposes of this paper my focus will be on distinctively Scottish developments though, in truth, the Scottish Committee of the Arts Council followed UK policies rather than a Scottish cultural agenda per se. When, for example, the desire for a Scottish Ballet Company emerged in the 1960s, Western Theatre Ballet was encouraged to move from Bristol to Glasgow to provide the Scottish company. In 1970 a report entitled 'Theatre in Scotland' considered moving Prospect Theatre Company from Bristol to become the Scottish National Theatre.[2]

These discussions are, of course, of their time but they do reveal the extent to which 'the arts' were viewed as a cultural tap to be turned on or off at will by the turn of subsidy, showering people with good things more or less regardless of social context or community traditions. This may be unsurprising given that Arts Council committees and offices were peopled with either 'cultural experts' from the high arts or those among the great and the good who liked to rub shoulders with creative and famous individuals.

What is more surprising is that Scottish local authorities followed this lead, without seriously examining the cultural fabric or interests of their own communities or electorates. The arts were subsidised in a slightly grudging yet unrationalised fashion, usually in isolation from other 'cultural' services such as libraries, museums and education.

The underlying presumption remained the need to improve people's cultural habits by applying appropriate high-art standards and experiences. Such standards were perceived as belonging to a deracinated aesthetic realm higher than local social mores.

This tenor became explicit in the attempts of the Arts Council and its Scottish Committee to distinguish between play-goers and theatre-goers. The former were seen as engaged in serious artistic activity worthy of subsidy, the latter indulging a suspect taste for popular entertainment. In 1961, the Scottish Committee instituted a bonus scheme for 'plays of good quality' to counter a perceived trend of Scottish theatres putting on popular shows to draw large attendances of theatre-goers. Given the long established traditions of popular theatre-going among working people in Scotland, this initiative reeks of class bias.[3] Yet the Arts Council would have been horrified by such an accusation; they were merely applying their normal canon of independent aesthetic values.

Of course, such policies depended on increasing public subsidies (the language of patronage had disappeared) at national and local levels. It needs a separate investigation to establish why the economic basis of cultural activity in Scotland had become so weak in the postwar period. Music, theatre, the visual arts and literature had all flourished in

Victorian and Edwardian Scotland with a mixed economy of popular appeal and patronage. Arts subsidies were now consciously applied to work against economic trends which were perceived as culturally deficient or harmful. It was not until the 1980s that people began gradually to speak of 'investing in' rather than 'subsidising' artistic activity.

In 1967, the Scottish Committee of the Arts Council of Great Britain became the Scottish Arts Council with a greater degree of independence and profile. It was still, however, part of the UK Arts Council and reported to Parliament via the London Council and the then Office of Arts and Libraries. This was all designed to protect the 'arm's length' principle separating politicians from cultural decisions. In this the arrangements were successful since, between 1967 and the Devolution Referendum in 1997, I cannot find any examples of a parliamentary question about the Scottish Arts Council, nor of the Scottish Arts Council giving evidence to a parliamentary committee. The first instance of this actually occurred between the 1997 Referendum and the elections for the first reinstated Scottish Parliament in 1999, when the Scottish Select Committee at Westminster grilled the Chair and Director of the Scottish Arts Council regarding the withdrawal of funding from Wildcat Theatre Company. By this time, the Scottish Arts Council had become fully independent of the former Arts Council of Great Britain and accountable to the Secretary of State for Scotland in the UK Cabinet.

This record, or non-record, of democratic debate regarding the publicly subsidised arts in Scotland is remarkable given the turbulence and controversy that beset arts organisations throughout the 1960s and 1970s. A socio-cultural revolution was taking place in attitudes to class, censorship and sexual morality, and to the role of explicit political discussion in culture. Such debates took place in the media with an unhealthy divide between the would-be debunkers of the popular press and the often uncritical advocacy of media commentators closely connected with the arts.

Nonetheless, despite the relatively protected position of the decision-makers, public debate about the rights and wrongs of funding decisions had begun; and arts organisations responded to social changes by diversifying to encompass political theatre, community arts, and arts in education. Later, ethnic minority arts and folk or traditional arts would be added to the repertoire of reports and programmes. In addition, throughout the 1970s, the relationship between the subsidised arts and Scottish cultural identity became a hot topic for debate. The lofty aesthetic realm was looking increasingly frayed and dragged down to earth.

Perhaps the most significant long-term trend of this period in Scotland was the growth in higher-education provision through the universities, the art colleges, and the Royal Scottish Academy of Music and Drama. Building on increased arts education at primary and secondary levels, a new generation of Scottish teachers, artists and writers emerged for whom the contemporary arts were integral to their emerging social contexts and identities. The rise of comprehensive education with increased access to the tertiary sector underpinned a marked narrowing of the gap between the arts and Scottish society as a whole.

These developments also laid the foundations for dramatic changes in the 1980s. The failure of the first Devolution Referendum in 1979, coupled with the onset of a Conservative administration led by Margaret Thatcher, politicised the arts in Scotland to a degree not previously experienced. Against the background of growing political and social frustration, cultural participation began to be seen as an expression of values and, effectively, of citizenship rather than solely an artistic experience.

Another aspect of the decade was the increasing dependence of arts organisations such as theatres on earned income, along with the realisation that the arts make a contribution to economic as well as social regeneration. These issues became acute in the urban lowlands as the closure of heavy industries led to unemployment and a raft of related social problems. It is therefore unsurprising that Glasgow led on this agenda with the Garden Festival in 1988 and the City of Culture designation for 1990. Local authorities, rather than solely an Arts Council, could now lead on culture.

It is easy to headline these changes by reference to high-profile initiatives but the underlying shift in perception is of equal, if not greater, interest. The publication of Alasdair Gray's influential novel *Lanark* in 1982 is a significant benchmark because it makes the representation of Scottish society in literature central to its theme; can Glasgow fully exist as a city until it has been created in the aesthetic realm? At another level, *Lanark* is a bildungsroman, tracing the trials of a young working-class Glaswegian who goes to art school and who seeks to apply the mainstream aesthetics to local society by painting murals in a church. Gray is, of course, himself an artist and onetime official painter to the city. On a third level, *Lanark* is explicitly political in the tradition of Orwell's *1984*, and of utopian/dystopian fantasies that comment ironically on the novel's realistic narrative strands. Gray's defining work is not only a masterly fictional achievement but a resounding integration of aesthetic concerns with Scottish social consciousness as a whole. The international recognition accorded to *Lanark* also adumbrates the increasing internationalisation of a distinctively Scottish cultural scene.

After a turbulent decade hanging precariously to the helm of a politically and culturally volatile vessel, the Scottish Arts Council moved itself in the 1990s into a period of significant change under the leadership of Seona Reid. The big shift in thinking was the recognition that partnership with other aspects and instruments of

Scottish society were central to the future health of the arts in Scotland; and that such partnership required shared understanding and decision-making. In partnership with the Convention of Scottish Local Authorities and the Scottish Museums Council, the Scottish Arts Council launched a 'Charter for the Arts in Scotland', in effect the biggest public consultation ever undertaken about the arts cultural provision across the country before the advent of the Scottish Parliament in 1999.

The tone of the whole exercise, ably summarised by Joyce McMillan, was positive, affirming widespread support for cultural activity of all kinds and the desire for further development. Among specifics were a demand for more support for the traditional arts and for an increase in distinctively Scottish theatre productions. The Scottish Arts Council sought to respond constructively to these demands. The benefit of such responsiveness in turn was that, in presenting the case for arts support, the Scottish Arts Council could now point to public demand and not just to its own strategic aspirations.[4]

Looking back with the benefit of hindsight, the charter process also marked an official widening of the purposes that investment in culture might serve. The trend towards citing social or economic benefits was emergent through the 1980s, but the Charter documentation and the responses embraced these different aspects of cultural activity in an inclusive way, while pointing to creative initiative and endeavour as the source of such benefits. The Scottish Arts Council had reinvented itself as a development agency offering expertise and advocacy, rather than solely (or even!) financial support, across the public sector.

These changes paved the way for new funding streams. In 1995, the Scottish Arts Council became a Lottery distributor with a doubling of disposable grant income. However, the range of potential beneficiaries and the spread of potential outcomes had increased exponentially as well.

Soon, virtually any area of public policy could justify arts funding on the basis that creativity could contribute to health, economic regeneration, learning skills, community development, social cohesion, youth justice, cultural diversity, conservation, heritage, environmental renewal, literacy, community safety, building design, to name a few! Arts administrators became adept at speaking a variety of languages, depending on the funder's objectives. The Scottish Arts Council was now like a charioteer with a big team of horses hopefully all pulling ultimately in the same direction.

A Scottish Parliament

The opening of the restored Scottish Parliament was greeted with enthusiasm by the cultural community. After all, had the artists, actors and writers not kept the flame of Scottish democracy alight – or so some liked to claim. However, in reality the first two parliamentary sessions of 1999–2003 and 2003–07 proved an exceptionally uncomfortable period for politicians and cultural workers alike.

One early development was a Parliamentary Committee enquiry into Scotland's national companies which embraced the concept of a Scottish National Theatre. This proved to be the first significant step in moving this long-held aspiration towards realisation with the launch in 2003 of a rapidly successful National Theatre of Scotland.

The first Scottish Executive led by Donald Dewar also acted quickly to produce a cultural policy entitled 'Creating the Future; Remembering the Past'.[5] However, while politicians were keen to be supportive and to put their stamp on cultural policy, they had no more idea of how to relate the arts to Scotland's newfound democratic accountability than the arts administrators. What ensued was an unanalysed slide on the political front into highlighting the social and economic benefits of arts investment, accompanied by increasing unease and distrust on the part of the cultural pundits.

A variety of political initiatives followed. On St Andrew's Day 2004, the then First Minister Jack McConnell gave a major speech at the Royal Scottish Academy of Music and Drama in Glasgow, setting out a vision of cultural access for all ages as the next great endeavour for public life in Scotland, and proposing the creation of a Cultural Commission.

Despite a rocky ride for the Commission, its final report did set out a sweeping vision for change. Amid its most important recommendations was the definition by law of cultural rights for all citizens, backed up by locally established and applied cultural entitlements. The citizens of Scotland had not, by and large, participated in this new charter process but it appeared to set their participation in the arts on a wholly new basis. Citizenship and culture were to be joined at the hip by law.[6]

However, neither government nor the political parties were convinced. The Scottish Executive came forward with its own policy, 'Scotland's Culture', and proceeded to consult on a draft Culture Bill. In this draft, the Executive's intention to exercise ultimate control over the decisions of its new cultural agency, Creative Scotland, was cruelly exposed to view, as was the muddle of cultural entitlements which had no defined cultural purpose and to which, in any case, no-one was entitled.

So, cultural policy limped into the second Scottish Election in 2007, in which the Labour Party was voted out of power in favour of a minority Scottish National Party administration.

The SNP government moved swiftly to establish overall strategic objectives for economic success and increased social justice. On the cultural front, the administration decided to postpone consideration of 'cultural entitlements' and to give local authorities freedom to decide on their own priorities and the extent to which culture might contribute to their delivery.

This minority government has also, as this book goes to press, brought forward a 'Creative Scotland' Bill, proposing a new cultural agency for the arts and the creative industries. There will be an active scrutiny process of the Bill, through the Education, Culture and Lifelong Learning Committee of the Scottish Parliament. A vigorous debate on objectives, definitions and priorities is anticipated. It will be interesting to see if, with a minority government, any party-political differences emerge over the relationship between citizenship and culture, and whether amendments to the Bill result.

Analysis

Where do these developments leave the relationship between citizenship and the arts? Also, how does that particular relationship figure within overall cultural environments?

Clearly, these issues have moved up the public agenda, in Scotland at least, and have engaged the devolved Parliament more than arts funding per se ever interested the UK Parliament at Westminster. However, the debate has been marred by (a) a confusion of purposes and (b) special interest pleading.

To take the latter first, the overwhelming majority of participants in these discussions were presenting their own sectoral interests. Many advanced good arguments on behalf of their art form, region or activity but largely failed to contribute to an overall framework of understanding. Objective research or consultation was at a premium, not least because the people with the vital specialist knowledge were those on the various cultural frontlines arguing their own case for resources.

This, of course, could have been anticipated and potentially contained if an underlying confusion of purpose had not continued to undermine public discussion and analysis. I would like, therefore to argue that there are four quite distinct areas that are served by public investment in culture and that, even when a particular initiative serves more than one, it is important to recognise the differences and apply different funding strategies.

First, there are economic purposes. All arts provision in Scotland since the 1960s has taken place against a background of increasing disposable income feeding leisure spending and consumer choice. Cultural investment is one way of meeting such demands and, in turn, stimulating employment, regional/national economic development and innovation.

This is a very wide field, ranging from tourism through to film, design and intellectual copyright. In growing economies these sectors are increasingly important in terms of competitiveness and high-value industries. Moreover, in all of these areas, private investors are the main players, while public funding is directed at influencing the share that any municipality, region or nation state can secure from increasingly globalised markets.

Surprisingly, Scotland has had, as yet, no coherent integrated investment plan in relation to either cultural tourism or what are variously termed the creative or cultural industries. Culture budgets are raided for economic purposes while economic development agencies view the cultural sector with some suspicion on the grounds that many of their activities are 'uneconomic'.

Second, there are what I would describe as cultural purposes in the social sense. These relate to how any social grouping invests in culture to express its identity, heritage and common values. At local, city, regional, and national levels, culture reflects a society to itself and to others. Often this is focused on particular institutions, buildings or locations. However such institutions, and governments at all levels, have worried increasingly since the 1980s about the degree to which citizens actually participate or engage. Hence emphasis on 'access' and 'inclusion'.

More recently, the trend in the public sector towards private sector models of management highlighting 'service delivery' and 'customer satisfaction' has challenged investment in institutions such as libraries, museums and theatres to justify public funding on the basis of quantitative results.

Naturally, there is overlap between the economic and socio-cultural dimensions but the latter cannot be reduced to the former, and the trend towards statistical measurement could undermine, as well as reinforce, longer-term strategic thinking.

To take just two examples – cultural diversity has become a critical issue because of major global challenges to social coherence in the United Kingdom. Arguments between so-called 'multiculturalists' and 'integrationists' demonstrate the high degree to which socio-cultural policies are driven by distinctively social aims and values. Likewise community regeneration – a favoured mantra in local government – is easy to map in terms of economic planning but much harder to realise in social terms. Cultural activity in the broadest sense may play a critical part in determining success or failure.

This also affects policy speak about 'Community Planning'. What in relation to community planning is Cultural Planning? Confusion here too is prevalent since there is a need to separate out the provision of cultural activities in a specific area from the way in which cultural dynamics can be built into planning processes. Good environmental design and social participation can work in creative partnership to achieve community health and well-being.

Third, there is the matter of education. Here the public sector in Scotland continues to be the main player while, in terms of citizenship, education alongside family culture retains a nearly universal influence. How do arts in their broader cultural context feature in recent developments in Scotland? In particular, how do they influence, and are in turn influenced by, the curriculum reforms which are currently engaging all those involved in Scottish education?

Of course, many of the competing purposes that impinge on culture press also on education. One of four keynote addresses at the 2007 Scottish Festival for Learning, the largest event on the national cultural calendar, featured Pasi Sahlberg, an education specialist from the World Bank. He identified climate change, digitalisation, global health risks and lifelong learning as some of the global issues which are driving curriculum development across different countries.[7]

This is fairly representative of a rhetoric of globalisation which is now frequently applied to drive change in the public sector, usually in the direction of 'economic efficiency'.

The reform process in Scotland, *A Curriculum for Excellence*, places its emphasis on the value of confident, creative individuals contributing effectively to society in the round. This reflects the strongly rooted humane values in Scotland which had a remarkable flourishing in the eighteenth-century Enlightenment.

Such humanism places a high value on intellectual enquiry and understanding as key to moral, psychological, social, economic, political, religious and aesthetic development. It also respects individual rights as foundational while emphasising social responsibilities. Though not all of Scotland's Enlightenment thinkers were democratic progressives, the working out of the Enlightenment agenda has led to democratic political reforms. All such progress, however, is based on advancing what David Hume described as 'the science of humanity' alongside the natural sciences.

In the broadest sense, therefore, curriculum reform in Scotland has a cultural context which is at least as important as its cultural or artistic content. This is a context which has much to offer internationally by resisting skills-based methodologies that lack intellectual or critical depth and so fail to equip citizens for democratic decision-making, or for a full and free expression of their humanity.

However, cultural and artistic content have also provoked some heated discussion. On St Andrew's Day 2005, the Literature Forum for Scotland petitioned the Scottish Parliament to recognise the right of all Scotland's citizens to have the opportunity to know something of the arts, literature, history and languages of Scotland. The Petition attracted extensive media coverage and widespread support.

Some educators regarded the Petition as defensively parochial while others wished to maintain the maximum freedom for the curriculum process without pressure from content-driven interest groups!

However, it is accepted pedagogy that children learn from their immediate environment and then, by extension and analogy, build understanding from their growing experience. It would therefore seem important that knowledge of local culture and history be a vital building block in any outward-looking curriculum. Since the capacity of individuals to contribute is based on critical understanding, this has to be grounded in self-critical awareness of the social and cultural environment in which learners are developing. These principles have been endorsed by the curriculum reform process in Scotland and what is emerging is a curriculum design in which the resources of Scotland's environment, history, literature, intellectual heritage, art and music will be harnessed to international perspectives. Any other outcome would hark back to periods when Scotland lacked confidence in its own cultural diversity or was constrained by the political perception that encouraging such diversity was to nurture nationalism.

Following the release of the Labour Executive's draft Culture Bill in 2006, the Literature Forum was again active in seeking to ally the notion of cultural entitlement with educational provision and lifelong learning. In the absence of any defined cultural purpose for such entitlements, the Literature Forum proposed two, one relating to cultural knowledge and one to aesthetic skills:

(a) To further an understanding of the history, literature, languages and arts of Scotland in their national and international contexts

(b) To develop appropriate skills in the appreciation and expression of creative language, music, movement and visual design.[8]

The second of these purposes clearly identifies an area of aesthetic knowledge and skills that enables individuals to actively shape the practice and understanding of artistic media. Passive reception fails the enquiry and understanding purpose of education as a whole. The Enlightenment framework also here recognises aesthetic perception as a distinctive kind of knowledge that requires distinctive skills of appreciation and expression. Such skills and knowledge do not, of course, exist in isolation within individuals or societies but they are in themselves necessary, if imagination is to have a social expression and contribute to wider understanding, enjoyment or well-being.

The purposes so proposed build a bridge between cultural entitlements in the wider social context and education. In doing this, they reflect a strong international commitment to humane values. They also affirm the integral point that artistic education plays in such a framework where it is seen as essential to a comprehensive education leading to the full development of the individual.

The Scottish National Party minority administration elected in 2007 has embedded these principles in its

Curriculum for Excellence guidance documents but has, so far, excluded any specific reference to Education from its draft Creative Scotland Bill.[9]

Fourth, in the light of the third point above, it is important to acknowledge distinctively aesthetic purposes in the formation of cultural policies and provision. This may seem self-evident but in reality cultural providers often marginalise this vital dimension by depicting it as 'art for art's sake', and then moving on to articulate social and economic purposes. A recent report on the state of the arts in Wales, for example, was summarised by its publishers, the Arts Council of Wales thus:

> A new digest documenting the state of the arts in Wales, confirms the increasing social and economic impact of the sector. Arts attendance has seen a steady growth over the past few years, with attendance rates increasing by 18% to 69% over the past decade. The creative industries are one of Wales's fastest growing economic sectors. Investment in creative buildings and events has been key to creating sustainable communities, with the construction of Galeri in Caernarfon and Wales Millennium Centre in Cardiff Bay both making a significant contribution to the regeneration of those areas.[10]

However, the importance of the aesthetic factor is not 'art for art's sake', a meaningless circular definition, but recognition that without the distinctively aesthetic the other much vaunted benefits are unobtainable. Aesthetic quality relates to excellence in conception and expression, in social and cultural contexts. It is not possible to separate the excellence or otherwise of aesthetic experience from its reception and appreciation. Equally, without the understanding and appreciation of the distinctive languages of artistic expression – visual design, music, movement and poetry – in society at large, the influence of art is strictly limited and potentially exclusive.

In the overall organisation of cultural provision, artists themselves need to be given space to articulate these values in order that clarity of purpose can be recovered. Societies need champions of imagination if aesthetic quality is to be nurtured and fully integrated into social, cultural and economic life through education and through the familial and public cultures.

A Conclusion about Citizenship

In this discussion I envisage citizenship as an expression of active participation that reaches beyond consumer choice to help shape the imaginative life of society. Such a citizen is both a critical appreciator and also, if desired, a creator. The right to exercise these roles is founded on lifelong arts education combined with access to the public cultural life of society. Such a citizen is positioned to make informed choices about cultural options.

There is a clear parallel between this mode of citizenship and participation in political understanding and decision-making, which is also grounded in universal education and the capacity for making informed choice. The expression of human freedom is political and cultural and often both together.

This parallel is in its turn central to a Scottish cultural heritage that is evolving in response to historical change, while sustaining continuity of human values and purpose.

Notes

1. Arts Council of Great Britain, *Annual Report* (London: ACGB, 1953), p. 2.
2. Donald Smith, '1950 to 1995', in Bill Findlay (ed.), *A History of Scottish Theatre* (Edinburgh: Polygon, 1978), pp. 28–78.
3. Ibid., p. 266.
4. Joyce McMillan, *Arts for a New Century* (Edinburgh: Scottish Arts Council, 1992) and *Charter for the Arts in Scotland* (Edinburgh: SAC, SMC, COSLA, 1993).

5. *Creating the Future; Remembering the Past* (Edinburgh: Scottish Executive, 1999).
6. *Our Next Major Enterprise: Final Report of The Cultural Commission* (Edinburgh: The Cultural Commission, 2005).
7. Festival for Learning, programme brochure (Glasgow: Learning and Teaching Scotland, 2007).
8. Evidence submitted by the Literature Forum for Scotland to the Scottish Executive Consultation on the Draft Culture Bill (Edinburgh: Scottish Executive, 2007).
9. Passim, http://curriculumforexcellence.scotland.gov.uk.
10. *The Arts Work: facts and figures 2007* (Cardiff: Arts Council Wales, 2007).

Trust and Trustworthiness in an Audit Society

Heidi Poon

Introduction

The best of children's stories often convey profound wisdom through simplicity, as is the case with Dr Seuss's Bee-Watcher fable.[1] What does a bee-watcher do? He keeps an eye on the lazy town bee, in the belief that being watched will make the bee work harder. When this does not produce the expected results, someone is appointed to keep an eye on the bee-watcher, until the whole town is engaged in a chain of supervision of a single lazy bee.

The bee-watching fable resonates with me as a chartered accountant qualified with one of the 'Big Four' in the 1990s. For a while, I was on the audit team of some of the blue-chip companies, and was seconded to a national service provider in its giant accounting and administration functions occupying an entire office block of some twenty-five storeys. As a junior in the audit team of a public listed company (plc), I was like a Bee-Watcher: the first link in a chain of monitoring. My work was reviewed by a supervisor, whose work was reviewed by an assistant manager, then by an audit manager, and then a senior audit manger, before it moved up to the partners' level. The review structure was like a pyramid, and the higher the review process moved up the levels, the further away it was from the ground – from those who were actually providing the services on the ground.

The service the bee is 'hired' to render is that of honey-making, and significantly, the primary activity of honey-making remains the exclusive art of the bee. However much the Bee-Watcher may *know* about honey making, he simply cannot produce honey as a bee can. The watcher of the bee-watcher, and the watcher of the watcher of the bee-watcher further represent this chain of displacement from the primary activity of honey-making.

The choice of having a bee to be watched by the whole town of watchers would appear to be far from random. As I read 'lazy bee', the phrase 'busy bee' keeps buzzing in my head, while another fable surfaces in my mind: that of the beautiful butterfly which flittered and fluttered away the summer months while the busy bee stored up honey for the winter. Surely, a bee cannot help but make honey. Making honey is the natural outflow of its ontological resources, as the psychologist may put it. However, a bee is not wont to be *driven* to work beyond its natural optimal; hence the watching procures no higher yield.

The fable finishes with the picture of a line of Bee-Watchers stretching to infinity, all dressed in the habit of a monk, some solemnly bowing their heads, some closing their eyes (for a nap?), and none but one with a smile on his face. The whole town ends up watching a bee! Absurdity, perversity, insanity! We laugh when we read it as a story, but – will we discern the absurdity if we meet it in reality?

My concern is that we may not, because our collective behaviour as citizens of a society often demonstrates the same inertia that allows a frog, if put in cold water to begin with, to be boiled alive eventually if that water is heated up slowly and gradually. The frog fails to discern that the gradual increase of the temperature of the water will become catastrophic to its own survival. 'Too comfortable with continuity to realise that continuous change at some point becomes discontinuous and demands a change in behaviour',[2] remarks Charles Handy in *Age of Unreason*. Handy draws the parallel between the inertia exhibited by the boiling frog to human behaviour to gradual changes on all levels: individual, organisational, social, national, international, and global.

In the fable of the Bee-Watcher, the escalating practice of watching happens *continuously* and *gradually* until the *discontinuous* situation is allowed to take place – that of the whole town being engaged in the business of watching. As a citizen in a profession, I am aware of the increasing burdens faced by many professions and public service workers, coming from compliance and regulations, from meeting the documentary requirements for quality assurance, from setting the timeframes and objectives of any initiatives to dovetail with the parameters of performance and funding assessments. Research assessment exercises, school inspection reports, league tables, hospital waiting lists, watchdog organisations, ... these are some of the indicators that our society is engaging itself in more 'watching' than it used to be. The increase of 'watching' in our society has been gradual but continuous. Will we be able to discern the point when the continuity becomes discontinuous, the point when absurdity reigns, in situations where the tail begins to wag the dog?

'A bee that is watched will work harder, you see' – and *this* is the assumption on which trust is built. Trust is placed, not on the bee, nor on the watchers, but in the function of watching. It is an assumption that raises two questions for me with relevance to citizenship education. First, what is the assumption upon which our society bases its trust? Second, how do we cultivate seeds of trustworthiness in growing citizens? This essay is an attempt to address these two questions and their implications for citizenship education.

Trust in an Audit Society?

There was a time when 'audit' was almost the exclusive practice of the financial sector. The subject of an audit was usually a set of accounts that required statutory disclosure to some third parties by law. An auditor was invariably a qualified accountant (in a pin-striped suit?). Good accounting practice is to record all the transactions of a business entity in such a way that the figures are rendered 'accountable' under certain prescribed headings in two prime statements: the profit and loss account, and the balance sheet. An accounting system is judged for its function in terms of the control measures in place that will ensure the *consistency*, *accuracy* and *completeness* in its recording of transactions. The figures behind any transaction should leave an 'audit trail' for the auditor to follow its moves through the accounting system from beginning to end.

Taking its model from financial auditing, the practice of audit spread phenomenally to all aspects of public life in Britain in the 1980s. It was no coincidence that the National Audit Office and the Audit Commission took their current form in 1983, with the express remit of addressing the 'economy, efficiency, and effectiveness' of all publicly funded activities within central and local government respectively. Public services such as hospitals, schools, universities, social and prison services, the police, are given performance targets to improve on their economy, efficiency and effectiveness. These targets are set in such a way that they can be audited, and meeting these targets becomes a governing force in service provision. In addition to financial and public services audits, the decade also witnessed the emergence of many new forms of auditing: environmental, value for money, management, forensic, data, intellectual property, medical, teaching, technology, stress, human rights, so much so that Michael Power's pithy title to his seminal treatise, *The Audit Explosion*, has become a popular byword for this phenomenon, and Britain has turned into what Power calls 'an audit society'.[3]

What then is perceived to be delivered by the audit process? The answers may include: independent assessment, objective monitoring, external verification, proper procedure, legislative compliance. What do these answers suggest of the *basis of trust* in an audit society? Though by no means conclusive, I believe that in an audit society, trust is being placed upon system controls and regulation compliance.

In other words, in an audit society, trust does not lie with the ground-workers (the bee), not even the monitoring bodies (the bee-watchers),[4] but with *the function of watching*. The apparent assumption that has led to the audit society can be put in the following terms: *the human worker that is audited will be more accountable*. By being 'accountable' in the auditing sense, the human agency becomes more controllable with reference to standards, more predictable in accordance with procedural protocol, more measurable in terms of performance targets, and freer from fraud and error, negligence and deviance. Are these the same criteria a mechanical engineer is after in assessing how good a piece of machinery is? The similarity is striking, and there is a sense that audit can bring human performance in line with mechanical performance.

'A bee that is watched will work harder' is the underlying assumption in the Bee-Watcher fable. 'A human worker that is audited will become more accountable' appears to be the underlying assumption that gives rise to the audit explosion. Trust is not placed in the human agency, but in the function of control designed to counter and contain the negative aspects whenever human agency is involved.

In the fable, does the bee work harder by being watched? No! In our audit society, what is the effect of audit on the workforce then? Unlike the bee, which remains nonchalant to any amount of watching, Power argues – powerfully – that the audit process itself, far from being a passive observer of performance, has turned into an *active* shaper of the practice it seeks to audit.[5] In an attempt to render professional and institutional practices auditable, the audit process has actually changed the way the ground-workers do their jobs. The parameters that set performance and efficiency targets begin to influence professional decisions: which patient to treat, which drug to prescribe, which suspect to prosecute, which pupil to suspend, which student to admit, which area of research to pursue, ... these are decisions, more often than not now, made with reference to some auditable parameters rather than on purely professional grounds. Studies into 'the mentality of the auditee' have shown that the growth of auditing and controlling measures on performance has led to a decline in organisational trust, an increase in defensive strategies, and a culture of blamism that stifles innovation and lowers employee morale.[6] As the audit process continues to shape the professional practices it audits, I would also add that the concept of *accountability* is increasingly displacing the concept of *responsibility* as the basis of trustworthiness.

Accountability and Trustworthiness

In an audit society where trust is placed in the function of control rather than in human agency, the corollary is to try to promote trustworthiness in human agency by holding the person to account through the audit process. People are to be rendered *accountable* in a performance audit in a similar fashion as numbers are made *accountable* in a financial audit. Given that performance audit has its origin in financial audit, it is not surprising that the concept of *accountability* has been grafted on to performance audit. However, the grafting of the term accountability on to human agencies can be insidious, in that it might have assumed too much familiarity between numbers and human agencies in the way they respond to the auditing process.

The shift further carries a transference in meaning. Numbers are rendered accountable by being explainable; human agencies are held accountable by being answerable for certain action. The financial auditing process has evolved to deliver the former meaning of accountability pertaining to numbers. Numerical figures that are made accountable can be 'pinned down' and 'followed' in an audit trail; figures can be quantified, specified, categorised and analysed. It remains highly questionable whether the latter meaning of accountability as applied to human agencies can be delivered by similar auditing procedure.

Not only is the affinity between what is *accountable* and what is *auditable* for numerical figures in a financial audit not immediately translatable in a performance audit, but I will further argue that even the financial audit process has two aspects: the technical and the judgemental. The technical aspects involve skills like sample testing, vouching of asset values by external means, verification of control mechanisms, accuracy of inputs and outputs, and so on. The judgemental aspects of the audit process are harder to quantify, and they require considerable business and financial acumen, experience, wisdom, foresight, and diplomacy to arrive at a 'true and fair' assessment. For example, should the auditor in the wake of the credit crunch advise a lender client to write off a much higher percentage of its 'borrowers' debts' as irrecoverable on prudence grounds? The consequences will be a drop in profit for the year, which will lead to a fall in the share price of the company. How much is the auditor going to exercise his prudence to press for a higher provision against the agenda of the Board of Directors, who are keener to maintain profit level and the share price?

When financial scandals make newspaper headlines, more often than not it is the judgemental aspects of the audit process that has missed the mark. In the example of Enron, it was the judgement that the 'partnership' entities (used by Enron to hide its debts and to exaggerate its earnings) were not subsidiary companies of Enron. The partnerships' accounts were therefore not consolidated into the group accounts of Enron. As a result of that judgement, year on year, the inflated earnings were imported into Enron's profit and loss account, and the debts stayed off its balance sheet.[7]

Furthermore, it is important to register that not only is human judgement involved in the audit process, but also that audit failure is usually located as a *particular* problem of fraudulent management in the business. Since the management problems are case-specific, it is equally important to realise that the legislation brought in to 'plug the hole' in the wake of an audit failure will not in itself preclude future audit failures from happening.

If reliance on audit is to minimise the need to place trust directly in human agency – by placing it on systems of control – we have to face up to the paradox that ultimately, we cannot avoid human agency. At some point along the chain of monitoring we are faced with human agency with all its fallibility. Much as we try to place our trust in control systems by legislating more auditing requirements, at some point in the auditing process, control systems recede to the background, and we are left with the auditor's judgement, and the management's integrity. The fact that even the audit process cannot bypass human agency is at the crux of the problems often referred to and the 'expectation gaps', between the public's perception that the auditor is there to detect fraud, and the auditor's remit to certify the soundness of control measures in place to vouch for the 'truth and fairness' of a set of financial statements.

Another level of 'expectation gaps' is perhaps more widely experienced, and less often makes newspaper headlines. The gaps exist between discharge accountability and service delivery. A quarter of a century after the audit explosion, *accountability* has become the ubiquitous term at the heart of any contractual relationships in public life. Holding the service providers to account appears to be the way to address 'trustworthiness' in the transactions. However, accountability is not synonymous with quality of services, because accountability is considered discharged when it can be demonstrated that systems of control and procedural measures are in place and observed. In health care, education, policing, for example, compliance procedure to discharge accountability has noticeably increased the administrative burden of those on the job, without necessarily improving the quality of services rendered.

In her BBC Reith lectures, Dame Onora O'Neill thinks that 'many public sector professionals find that the new demands (of compliance procedure) damage their real work'. She highlights the bane of a compliance culture where:

> Professionals have to work to ever more exacting – if changing – standards of good practice and due process, to meet relentless demands to record and report, and they are subject to regular ranking and restructuring.[8]

Furthermore, in a culture of accountability, blameworthiness rather than trustworthiness seems to have been promoted. When people are held to account in their jobs, they become defensive rather than proactive. O'Neill speaks of the 'new accountability' as 'widely experienced not just as changing', but in her opinion, 'as distorting the proper aims of professional practice and indeed as damaging professional pride and integrity'. She refers to a 'crisis of public trust' in which professionals and public servants are now *perceived* to be less trustworthy, and that we are 'heading towards defensive medicine, defensive teaching and defensive policing'. This resonates with Power's assertion in his seminal thesis on *Audit Explosion*: that the spread of audit, instead of promoting trust, 'creates the very distrust it is meant to address'.

Writing with reference to 'the accountability problems' in education, Luvern Cunningham offers us an insight into why 'the politics of accountability is an exceedingly tricky domain' – because 'it is difficult to sort out those phenomena that are essentially political from those that are organisational'.[9] Perfect accountability appears to be a will-o'-the-wisp, nor does it deliver the Holy Grail of trustworthiness. In our quest for 'greater accountability', which is an honourable political aim, we run the danger of allowing 'the triumph of bureaucracy over democracy'. Apart from the burden of bureaucracy, it is also questionable whether 'programmatic commitments to greater accountability' actually contributes to transparency and democracy. Power answers emphatically in the negative with substantive evidence in his book *The Audit Society*.[10] Citing Day and Klein, he recommends 'a civic dialogue to create at least something of the high visibility and directness of the face to face accountability'.[11]

It drives home the fact that in a democracy, the political relevance of some form of accountability cannot be bypassed. But if the culture of accountability is not engendering trustworthiness, we need to rethink how we can nurture trust in our society. Leslie Lipson in *Democratic Civilisation* puts forward a question which serves as a good starting point for this concluding section: 'All democracies have to cope with a contradiction which is inherent in power itself: if used, it may be abused. How does one provide for the former and prevent the latter?' The consideration of this question is 'at the heart of the problem of responsibility',[12] and the focus of the final section of this essay.

Responsibility and Responsiveness

'If children live with trust, they will turn out to be trustworthy' is such an old adage that it may sound like an cliché to some. Earlier in this essay, I have mentioned that 'accountability' is increasingly displacing 'responsibility' as the basis of trust. If we are wont to hold children to account, they may learn how to fulfil the duties and be law-abiding, step into their roles, but will they learn to trust themselves, become trustworthy and able to trust others? The relationship between trusting ourselves and trusting others is a complex one. I believe we need to nurture the sense of *responsibility* as the basis of self-trust, and trustworthiness and trust in others.

Response-ability is the ability to respond, to be an active agent in one's undertaking, to know one has been trusted with a duty that one wants to honour. In growing the citizens of the next generations, we need to nurture the seeds of responsibility (the ability to respond) that I believe is innate in each of us. Simone Weil refers to responsibility as a vital need of the soul:

> Initiative and responsibility, to feel one is useful and even indispensable, are vital needs of the human soul.... For this need to be satisfied it is necessary that a man should often have to *take decisions* in matters great or small affecting interests that are distinct from his own, but in regard to which he feels a personal concern. He also requires to be continually called upon to supply fresh efforts. Finally, he requires to be able to encompass in thought the entire range of activity of the social organism to which he belongs, ... For that, he must be made acquainted with it, be asked to interest himself in it, be brought to feel its value, its utility and, where necessary, its greatness, and made fully aware of the part he plays in it.[13]

I take the view that autonomy, the ability to *take decision*, as so emphasised in Weil's view, is the *sine qua non* of a responsible self. The concept of accountability seeks to control the passive self in human agency, while the sense of responsibility empowers the active self to be autonomous. It is only when one can be autonomous that one can become responsive, in both creativity and initiative.

In our audit society, dominated by the culture of accountability, what does it mean to turn the soil round so that we may sow seeds of responsibility? The following thoughts are not prescriptive, but to start raking the soil for a culture of responsibility to take root, certain notions associated with the audit society need to be addressed in citizenship education: and serve more as pointers for further reflection on where seeds of changes may be sown.

1. Cultivate an awareness of what audit is supposed to deliver. The so-called expectation gaps need to be publicly acknowledged and accepted.
2. To understand that it is in its failure that the audit function gets noticed; and that the response to call for higher level of regulatory audit does not in itself prevent future failures.
3. However much we want to minimise the risk in trusting human agency by putting trust in systems of control, we cannot bypass human agency in the end. An element of risk is inevitable therefore, however extensive the control measures that are in place.
4. Risk can never be completely eliminated; perfect accountability is a will-o'-the-wisp. If society remains highly risk-averse, it will call for more audit. The absurdity of the bee-watching town or the frog boiled to death are reminders that continuous practice can become discontinuous. A healthy and even attitude towards risk is essential to maintain a sense of balance.

5. Our audit culture has promoted values that can be measured in terms of output quantifiable in numerical or monetary values, and this has affected the values of certain subjects in our educational system too. It is important to recognise that growing responsible and responsive citizens will not be met by citizenship education as narrowly defined in the syllabus.

To grow 'responsible and responsive' citizens requires the support of the range of subjects that comes under the nature of values embodied in arts and humanities. The values of arts and humanities may not be measured in monetary terms. Their values lie in nurturing creativity, cultivating empathy, developing sociality in discourse, building a cultural tradition for civic engagement, and above all, in developing the moral imagination that underpins wisdom. In the words of an educationalist: 'Only very basic skills, like reading and mathematics, could be specified in such a precise behavioural manner. Other aims, like ... becoming a good citizen, were much more difficult to turn into observable behaviour.'[14]

Let these be the last words. Success in growing responsible and responsive citizens is certainly not going to be 'auditable'.

Notes

1. Dr Seuss, *Did I ever tell you how lucky you are?* (New York: Random House, 1973).
2. Charles Handy, *The Age of Unreason* (London: Arrow Books, 1990), p. 8.
3. Michael Power, *The Audit Explosion* (London: Demos, 1996). The 53-page document is on open access at http://www.demos.co.uk.
4. See the examples of subjecting the Inland Revenue Inspection or the police force to 'value-for-money' audit, or the regime of 'auditing the auditor' under the requirements of the Eighth

European Directive on company law, cited in Power, *The Audit Explosion*, p. 11.

5. See Michael Power, 'Evaluating the Audit Explosion', in *Law and Policy* (July 2003), pp. 185–202, pp. 188–91.
6. See Power, ibid., p. 190 and the cited references.
7. See, for example, Ronald R. Sims and Johannes Brinkmann, 'Enron Ethics (Or: Culture Matters More than Codes)', in *Journal of Business Ethics* 45 (2003), pp. 243–56.
8. Onora O'Neill, 'Called to Account' in BBC Reith lectures, 2003. http://www.bbc.co.uk/radio4/reith2002/lecture3.shtml (accessed June 2008).
9. Luvern L. Cunningham, 'Our Accountability Problems', in *Theory into Practice* (October 1969), pp. 285–92, p. 290.
10. Michael Power, *The Audit Society: Rituals of Verification*, (Oxford: Oxford University Press, 1997), p. 13.
11. Patricia Day and Rudolf Klein, *Accountabilities: Five Public Services* (London: Tavistock, 1987), p. 249; quoted in Power, *Audit Explosion*, p. 21.
12. Leslie Lipson, *The Democratic Civilization* (New York: Oxford University Press, 1964), p. 478, quoted in William S. Livingston, 'Britain and America: The Institutionalization of Accountability', in *Journal of Politics* (November 1976), pp. 879–94, p. 890.
13. Simone Weil, *The Need for Roots* (London: Routledge, 1952), p. 15. Italics mine.
14. William R. Johnson, 'A Vision Not a Viewpoint' in *Theory into Practice* (December 1979), pp. 327–87, p. 380.

Reasserting the Politics of Democratic Citizenship[1]

Ian Martin

The Primacy of Politics

> The way we define citizenship is intimately linked to the kind of society and political community we want. (Chantel Mouffe 1992)[2]

The argument starts from the assertion that citizenship is primarily a political category. For Aristotle, the citizen was 'someone who participates in public affairs', by definition a 'political animal'. Whatever else it may be (and in a democracy we can, and must, argue about that), citizenship expresses our status as members of a political community – and our rights and responsibilities to act and to be accountable as agents within the politics of the state.

Citizens are people who make and respond to political arguments and who make political choices. And if citizenship is primarily a political category, it is important not to shy away from the politics of citizenship and the conditions in which we are expected to act as citizens. In this sense, thinking about citizenship is one way of beginning the larger task which is, in Zygmunt Bauman's words (1999),[3] to 're-invent politics', a process which has to be 'cared for and cultivated in company with others'. Implicit in this is the view that the political expression of citizenship is fundamentally a moral activity in which we collectively argue about the relationship between means and ends. Without this constant and continuous re-invention of the political, societies become morally bankrupt. It is essential for the health of democracy that the educational space for this creative, democratic work be cherished and expanded.

And yet, it seems to me that education for citizenship today is often presented as quite the opposite of this: a sanitised and diversionary discourse – almost a way of *not* talking about politics and political choices. I recently read in yet another worthy but turgid tome about such things that this effect is termed 'depolitico-ideologisation'! Where there is no democratic argument, the public business of the citizen is impoverished and reduced to the privatised transaction of the customer. Indeed, one of the problems with the 'end of ideology' managerialism of New Labour is that what we really need is more ideology and more political argument, not less.

All the literature tells us that citizenship is an 'essentially contestable concept'. In a democracy citizenship is constituted and reconstituted in the continuing political debate over what it means and how its meaning changes over time.

Three Dimensions of Citizenship

T. H. Marshall (1950)[4] famously distinguished between the *civil*, *political* and *social* axes of citizenship. Civil rights refer to our freedoms under the law, political rights to our participation in the democratic process, and social rights to our enjoyment of the basic conditions of life which make being a citizen meaningful and worthwhile. These rights have, of course, been fought and struggled for over the centuries; and their gradual extension has been erratic and uneven – always wrested by the 'have-nots' in the teeth of opposition from the 'haves'. Marshall went on to argue for a composite and distinctively modern form of citizenship based on the relationship between our legal, political and welfare rights and responsibilities. It is the proper balance between these different axes of citizenship which must be maintained if citizenship is to remain meaningful as, in Marshall's words, a 'status bestowed on all those who are full members of a community'.

Marshall's tripartite account is still a good way to begin thinking about citizenship because it helps us to understand not only the distinctive components of citizenship but also their interdependence and the balance between them. In this respect, it is important to note the crucial role of progressive social policy in managing the inherent contradictions of 'democratic-welfare-capitalism' because 'the social rights embedded in the institutions of the Welfare State are essential to minimise those social and economic inequalities which are incompatible with the civil and political equality that positive participation requires' (Carr and Hartnett 1996).[5] The question is: how is the balance between the civil, political and social axes of citizenship differentially inscribed in the lives of citizens today?

Of course, Marshall's account has been extensively critiqued, partly because of its gender- and colour-blind assumptions. In consequence and as part of the democratic debate, we should listen carefully to arguments coming from feminists and disabled people about care and citizenship. Any inclusive notion of citizenship must recognise a non-gendered 'ethics of care' as a key dimension of citizenship, i.e. as a civic virtue which is equal and complementary to the dominant and almost entirely economistic ethic of paid work. Otherwise, there is a danger of citizenship operating as much as a mechanism of exclusion as inclusion.

I would contend that increasingly, in Marshall's terms, the social (as distinct from the civil and political) rights of citizenship within the public domain of the state are being stripped away – to be recovered and reconstituted, if possible, within the private domain of work, family and community. For example, the dominant discourse of lifelong learning today seems to be essentially about learning to be self-sufficient (and self-interested) citizens – as if that is not a contradiction in terms. Indeed, it can be argued that lifelong learning, in this sense, is *the* crucial agent of the civic remoralisation that is at work within the modernising project of New Labour. It is in terms of what lifelong learners are expected to learn that the *de*construction of welfare is predicated upon the *re*construction of citizenship (see Martin, 2003).[6] In the process, the balance between our individual status as citizens and our collective practice of citizenship, or what Lister (1997)[7] calls 'formal' and 'substantive' citizenship, is being actively redrawn and skewed.

This distinction between citizenship as status and citizenship as practice is important – and somewhat neglected in current discussions. As our society becomes more unequal and atomised, we need to be thinking much more seriously about what citizens can expect as well as what can be expected of citizens. Current proposals for 'education for citizenship', for instance, seem to be preoccupied with the exercise of individual rights and responsibilities – increasingly, in fact, with *duties and responsibilities* – and to be wilfully silent about the social and material conditions in which it is reasonable to expect citizens to be active members of the political community. And yet the practice of citizenship, and the democratic argument about what it means, goes on in every single struggle against poverty, injustice, discrimination and exclusion. So, perhaps we should be asking how education can support the social practice of citizenship and resource the collective struggles of citizens (and, indeed, non-citizens) as well as prepare individuals for the formal status of citizenship.

We also have to understand, of course, that the very notion of 'liberal democracy' embodies a potential contradiction between its moral and market elements – and that this has very different consequences for different people. Indeed, one of the fundamental problems in today's globalised 'New World Order' is the tendency to lose sight of this and to conflate democracy with the market system.

Three Ways of Thinking about Education and Citizenship

What do citizens need to know, and know about? It is useful to distinguish between three ways of thinking about education and citizenship: procedural, substantive and contingent.

First, the *procedural* approach concerns citizens' participation in the democratic process. This is the familiar discourse of political rights and duties, largely articulated within the notion of citizenship as status. What is required is relatively specialised knowledge about political means – how the system works.

Second, the *substantive* approach concerns the willingness and ability of citizens to engage in political argument about the nature and purposes of public life. Essentially, this concerns what citizens need to know about the substantive business of politics in order to join in the argument. What is required is relatively generalised understanding about political ends – what the system is for.

Third, the *contingent* approach concerns the wider circumstances in which citizens feel that they are 'full members of a community' and, as a consequence, may reasonably be expected to be active and engaged in both procedural and substantive terms. One of the things this suggests is that education is no panacea when we confront the problems and possibilities of citizenship in any particular situation. In this sense, education is, at best, a necessary rather than a sufficient condition of citizenship. It also suggests that it is nearly always important to reassert the politics of citizenship.

Most current discussion seems to be about the procedural and, to a lesser degree, substantive approaches to education for citizenship. My own focus of interest, however, is on what I have called the contingent approach. We have to be clearer about the *non*-educational preconditions for citizenship and the broader social context in which people are encouraged or discouraged to act as citizens. It has become fashionable to talk about citizenship in terms of a shared sense of 'belonging', 'identification' and 'rootedness'. What are people being asked to belong to, to identify with, to be rooted in? To what extent does their individual experience yield a common sense of a common citizenship? Ralph Miliband (1994)[8] reminds us that true citizenship presupposes a 'rough equality of condition' and, indeed, that 'equality of opportunity is a mere slogan in societies marked by deep inequalities of condition'. And, of course, we live in just such a society. This means that if we are really interested in education for citizenship, we need to start *outside* the education system.

The Quality of Public Life

Thinking about the wider context of citizenship involves a consideration of the *non*-educational preconditions of informed and active citizenship. We must also think very carefully about what education can and cannot be expected to do – always bearing in mind A. H. Halsey's salutary warning that, all too easily, education becomes the 'waste paper basket of social policy'. So, what does the public life of the community feel like today? I confine myself to a series of questions, followed by some very brief comments.

Do we organise our public goods in ways that promote the public good? Our railways seem to epitomise the problem: to put it bluntly, here we have a privatised public service which simply doesn't work (except for the fat cats, of course – who don't travel by rail, anyway). Has it ever occurred to you as you sit – or, indeed, stand – in a crowded train which has, inexplicably, come to a halt in the middle of nowhere that you would prefer to be addressed over the loudspeaker as a 'passenger' as distinct from a 'customer'? Then, at least they might remember that you are on a train because you actually want to get somewhere.

Do we arrange our public life in ways which encourage trust and reciprocity among citizens? We hear a lot in New Labour-speak about the importance of 'social capital', but we see much less evidence of any serious attempt to create the conditions for the generation of social capital. Indeed, the obsession with presentation and 'spin', which has now come to haunt New Labour, has had the effect of actually putting many ordinary (and sensible) people off politics, i.e. actively to de-activate them as citizens. The managerialist state suffocates the politics of citizenship.

Is choice a substitute for welfare? Most people, surely, don't want to choose between hospitals and schools; they simply want good, reasonably accessible hospitals and schools. In this kind of transaction, they want to be citizens – not customers or merely consumers. We really do seem to be living in an accountant's world in which we know the cost of everything and the value of nothing. I want to emphasise three points: first, it is in the ways we order our social institutions that we either express the common bonds of a common citizenship or succumb to what Habermas (1996)[9] calls the 'syndrome of civic privatism' (which is, essentially, the enemy of democratic citizenship); second, this is not about government doing things for people – it is about citizens demanding that government does what it's for; third, as Richard Titmuss argued, a fundamental principle of public (or what he called 'institutionalised') welfare is to minimise the conflict, inevitable in human affairs, between egoism and altruism.

What is the place of the 'other' in our social and political life? The very idea of citizenship tests suggests the extent to which the dominant discourse of citizenship has become a pathological discourse. Problems and deficits and dangers are always located in the disaffected, apathetic or alien 'other'. In reality, what most migrants, refugees and asylum seekers want most is simply to be good, active and productive citizens – and the education and opportunity to become such citizens (see Bellis and Morrice 2003).[10]

Does all the talk about 'inclusion' and 'exclusion' really gets to grips with what is going on? It seems to me that if we are seriously interested in democratic citizenship, we really need to revisit the old ideas of social justice and equality. But if we have to use the politically correct terminology of 'inclusion' and 'exclusion', let us do so in a more discriminating and even-handed way. As Ruth Lister (2001)[11] emphasises, social exclusion works both ways:

> What is at issue is not just the exclusion from the bonds of common citizenship of those at the bottom, but also the way in which those at the top can exclude themselves from these bonds and thereby fail to acknowledge the equal worth of their fellow citizens.

Cosmopolitanism, Citizenship and Justice: Stretching the Discourse

I have argued that part of the educational task is to examine the conditions in which we are expected to act as citizens, and the extent to which these confer upon us the common sense of a common citizenship. In doing so, we must never forget that democracy cannot do without the dissenting citizen – or that education has its part to play in preparing citizens for democratic dissent. At the same time, we must also begin to think much more seriously and ambitiously about our citizenship of the world. In doing so, we might start with the question posed by that great and radical thinker, Edward Said, in an interview shortly before his untimely death: 'Why does no one mention truth and justice any more?' This, he believed, is what nearly everyone, nearly everywhere wants. Perhaps it is also where our interest in education and citizenship should really begin – and end.

If we are still seriously interested in the big ideas like truth, justice and democracy, we must learn to think outside the increasingly small box of the policy and politics of the nation state. In a recent paper called 'Reframing justice in a globalised world', Nancy Fraser contends that 'the grammar of the argument has altered' (Fraser 2005).[12] The idea of 'reframing' helps to stretch our thinking towards a more cosmopolitan understanding of citizenship and social justice.

Fraser argues that within the historically specific context of the twentieth-century nation state, justice was initially defined primarily in material terms: the key issues related to *(re)distribution*, and these were mediated through a modernist politics of class. More recently, this paradigm has been progressively challenged (supplemented rather than replaced) by notions of justice defined in cultural terms: the key issues related to *(mis)recognition*, and these were mediated through a postmodern politics of identity and difference. In both cases, however, the discussion was framed within the problems and possibilities of the national/territorial state. Globalisation, however, radically qualifies traditional notions of sovereignty, and calls for a more cosmopolitan framing of the issues in a way that recognises a third dimension of justice. This adds the issue of political *representation* to those of material distribution and cultural recognition. But political representation now has to be understood and enacted outside as well as inside the traditional politics of the state. Using Manuel Castells' terminology, Fraser argues that one of the consequences of globalisation is that many of 'the forces that perpetuate injustice belong to not the "space of places", but the "space of flows"'.

Cosmopolitanism has been defined as a 'sensibility predicated on a willingness to step outside oneself in order to engage the other in a substantive and meaningful way', and it can be argued that globalisation creates the 'objective conditions for a new cosmopolitan pedagogy' (Bronner 2004).[13] The task of building such a pedagogy seems to me to be a real challenge for a new and cosmopolitan (as distinct from simply international) educational movement for democratic citizenship.

It was thinking along these lines that recently encouraged some of us working in adult education and community development in Scotland to circulate an 'Open letter: Whatever happened to learning for democracy?' This read as follows:

> We see our work in community-based education as part of a broader democratic process. This is about enabling people to demand social justice and equality for themselves and others. There is now an historic opportunity to renew democracy in Scotland, and yet we are beginning to feel a profound sense of disappointment about the way in which both our own work and the lives of people in communities are being managed, regulated and controlled.
>
> Community learning is being tied into state policy rather than policy being informed by democratic learning. Despite much good practice on the ground, there is a systematic and debilitating reductionism at work in the policy agenda: lifelong learning is largely reduced to instrumental and economistic terms, to learning for a living rather than learning for life; community development is largely reduced to delivering the community to policy through pseudo-democratic forms of participation and partnership; working with young people is largely reduced to surveillance and

> preparation for employment. There can be no vision of a different kind of Scotland in this systematic reduction of democratic purpose to managerial procedure.
>
> This is not the way to activate citizens for democratic renewal or enthuse them about the possibilities of democratic life. Moreover, there is a real danger of a new kind of democratic deficit developing. The real threat to Scotland's new democracy comes not from apathy but from cynicism.
>
> What is required, in the first instance, is a much more open, democratic and imaginative dialogue and debate about what kind of society we want to live in, and how we can begin to build it in Scotland today. Education and learning in communities can contribute to making this vision a reality, and they are a rich resource for tackling significant problems in society. Ordinary people need the opportunity to have their say, to be listened to and to talk back to the state. This is essentially a democratic process. It cannot simply be managed and measured; it has to be nurtured and cultivated in communities. It requires faith and trust in the people, and a valuing of genuinely democratic dialogue and debate.

This obviously struck a chord because it stimulated a great deal of interest and support, leading to a considerable amount of discussion and activity. One outcome of all this is a summary document which has been produced in the form of a laminated wall chart which is specifically designed to be displayed in classrooms, offices and public places. It represents the idea of 'learning for democracy' in terms of ten propositions (statements of principle) and ten proposals (statements for action). The intention is to rekindle the democratic impulse, which we believe should be at the heart of our work in community-based education and development. These propositions and proposals about learning for democracy seem a fitting way to conclude this argument about putting the politics back into democratic citizenship.

Learning for Democracy: Ten Propositions

Democracy is about:

1. Freedom

Human flourishing is achieved through freedom to act individually and collectively, only constrained by due consideration for others.

2. Equality

All people are of the same moral worth and are obliged to mind the equality of others.

3. Justice

Justice and democracy are interdependent. An unjust society is an undemocratic society and an undemocratic society breeds injustice.

4. Solidarity

Shared aims and values arise from the pursuit of common purposes and mutually supportive ways of living.

5. Diversity

Dialogue between different cultures and identities can enrich society and help to build a common culture.

6. Accountability

The state is accountable to its citizens for providing the policy framework within which judgements about the common good are made and contested. Those who hold power are answerable to the people.

7. Dialogue

Democracy requires dialogue and the possibility of dissent. This means learning to argue, articulate beliefs, deliberate and come to collective decisions concerning what constitutes the good society.

8. Responsibility

Consistency and coherence between private and public behaviour are essential to the quality of democratic life.

9. Participation

Democracy is something to be negotiated from below rather than handed down from above. Citizens require the opportunity to talk back to the state.

10. Sustainability

A commitment to the environment and to future generations requires determined opposition to those forces which are wasteful and destructive.

Learning for Democracy: Ten Proposals

Learning for democracy means:

1. Taking sides

Educational workers are not merely enablers or facilitators. The claim to neutrality can reinforce and legitimise existing power relations. Practitioners need to be clear about what they stand for – and against.

2. Acting in solidarity

Practitioners should proactively seek opportunities to engage in a critical and committed way with communities and social movements for progressive social change.

3. Taking risks

Critical and creative learning is necessarily unpredictable and open-ended. Exploring official problem definitions and challenging taken-for-granted ways of thinking can be a liberating process.

4. Developing political literacy

Politics needs to be made more educational and education made more political. Learning to analyse, argue, cooperate, and take action on issues that matter requires a systematic educational process.

5. Working at the grassroots

Democracy lives through ordinary people's actions; it does not depend on state sanction. Practitioners should be in everyday contact with people on their own ground and on their own terms.

6. Listening to dissenting voices

Activating democracy is a process of creating spaces in which different interests are expressed and voices heard. Dissent should be valued rather than suppressed.

7. Cultivating awkwardness

Democracy is not necessarily best served by the conformist citizen. This means that the educational task is to create situations in which people can confront their circumstances, reflect critically on their experience and take action.

8. Educating for social change

Collective action can bring about progressive change. Learning for democracy can contribute to this process by linking personal experience with wider political explanations and processes.

9. Exploring alternatives

Learning for democracy can provide people with the opportunity to see that the status quo is not inevitable – that 'another world is possible'.

10. Exposing the power of language

The words used to describe the world influence how people think and act. Learning for democracy involves exploring how language frames attitudes, beliefs and values.

Notes

1. The first part of this chapter was originally published as 'Putting politics back into citizenship' in *Adults Learning* 15, 4 (December 2003).
2. C. Mouffe (ed.), *Dimensions of Radical Democracy: pluralism, citizenship, community* (London: Verso, 1992).
3. Z. Baumann, *In Search of Politics* (Cambridge: Polity Press, 1999).
4. T. H. Marshall, *Citizenship and Social Class* (Cambridge: Cambridge University Press, 1950).
5. W. Carr and A. Hartnett, 'Civic education, democracy and the English tradition', in J. Demaine and H. Entwistle (eds), *Beyond Communitarianism: citizenship, politics and education*, (Basingstoke: Macmillan, 1996).
6. I. Martin, 'Adult education, lifelong learning and citizenship: some ifs and buts', *International Journal of Lifelong Education* 22, 6 (2003).
7. R. Lister, *Citizenship: Feminist Perspectives* (Basingstoke: Macmillan, 1997).
8. R. Miliband, *Socialism for a Sceptical Age* (Cambridge: Polity Press, 1994).
9. J. Habermas, *Between Facts and Norms: Contributions to a discourse theory of law and democracy* (Cambridge, MA: MIT Press, 1996), p. 78.
10. A. Bellis and L. Morrice, 'A sense of belonging: asylum seekers, cultural difference and citizenship', in P. Coare and R. Johnston (eds), *Adult Learning, Citizenship and Community Voices* (Leicester: National Institute of Adult Continuing Education, 2003).
11. R. Lister, 'New Labour: a study in ambiguity from a position of ambivalence', *Critical Social Policy* 21, 4 (2001).
12. N. Fraser, 'Reframing justice in a globalised world', *New Left Review* 36 (2005).

13. S. E. Bronner, *Reclaiming the Enlightenment: Towards a Politics of Radical Engagement* (New York: Columbia University Press, 2004).